SOUTHERN WAY
THE OTHER SIDE OF THE SOUTHERN

Special

Accidents, Incidents & Occasions
Compiled by Kevin Robertson

© Kevin Robertson (Noodle Books) and the various contributors 2012

ISBN 978-1-906419-80-6

First published in 2012 by Kevin Robertson
under the **NOODLE BOOKS** imprint
PO Box 279
Corhampton
SOUTHAMPTON
SO32 3ZX

www.noodlebooks.co.uk
editorial@thesouthernway.co.uk

Printed in England by
Ian Allan Printing Ltd
Hersham, Surrey

Publishers note: Every effort has been made to identify and correctly annotate photographic credits. Should an error have occurred then this is entirely unintentional.

Front cover - *No. 34057 'Biggin Hill' showing the effects of an oil-bath fire which occurred near Hamble Halt, 22 May 1961. See also page 27 and Issue No 4 of 'The Southern Way'.*

Roger Holmes

Rear cover - *EMUs in trouble Top left - The consequences of an EMU trying to go into two platforms at once at Horley (the signalman reversed the Down end crossover under the train. After the event one of the vehicles is seen with an accommodation bogie under one end, as Viv Orchard points out, "...this probably accounts for the rough riding of these units.!" The other three views are at Guildford shortly after EPB brakes had been introduced. A driver error resulted in the train over-running platform one with unfortunately fatal consequences for the Guildford Station master in the office at the end of the platform.*

Viv Orchard

Title page - *The approach to Waterloo, 28 September 1966. The damaged front end of 2HAL unit No. 2626 after its head on collision with Class 2 No. No 82023. See also pages 96 and Issue No. 2 of 'The Southern Way'.*

Andy Gibbs/ Pete Beyer

Pages 2/3 - *On 14 October 1951, 'K' class 2-6-0 No. 32347 was severely damaged when it 'ran away' from Bricklayers Arms and came into collision with the tender of 'L' No. 31741 at Rotherhithe Road. The tender of the 'L' was destroyed, a replacement, it is believed, being found ex No. 31545. Despite the considerable damage suffered by the 'K' it was inspected after being towed to Brighton was considered worthy of repair which task was undertaken at Eastleigh. It is seen here temporarily back at Bricklayers Arms and would survive in service until 1962.*

INTRODUCTION

The subject of accidents, be it rail, road or other form of travel holds a peculiar fascination to most.

Yes, there will be the occasional sad individual whose twisted mind actually gains pleasure at the misfortune of others, yet for the rest of us mortals we are content to watch from the sidelines, to slow down and gawp at the twisted wreckage on the side of a motorway, whilst complaining bitterly at everyone else who does the same thing in front of us rather than 'getting a move on'.

I have never been involved in a railway accident, car accident yes - not an experience I would wish to repeat, whilst in a past life I was charged with picking up the pieces following those same motorway accidents referred to previously.

Nowadays when it all goes wrong, be that road or rail, the route is closed for hours or days: blame it seems must be apportioned, and until it can be hung around someone or something's neck, nothing will move.

How different to days even within living memory. Then the priority was not the investigation, instead it was the restoration of traffic - ensuring the customer or goods reached his destination with the minimum of delay.

Accidents and incidents are a fact of life. Designers, engineers and the like have tried their best to improve safety over the 150+ years since the advent of the railway and in so doing achieved much. No doubt further advances will be made as the years pass , advances which we today cannot even begin to imagine.

But one common factor exists in nearly every accident and that is the human element. Often a single simple error or lapse of concentration leads to a compound error and the result is a derailment - or worse.

Reverting back to the start of this page I commented that the subject is railway accidents, indeed it is, but deliberately not those where carnage and serious loss of life has occurred. Hence locations such as Lewisham, Hither Green, and Clapham are deliberately excluded. Further back in time we may instead look at the occurrences at Gomshall and St Johns, to name but two, but the majority of this work is deliberately aimed at things that bumped, dented, broke, and fell off, none deliberate but they happened all the same. Consequently whilst undoubtedly there will have been some human trauma involved, it is to be hoped this will be seen in the light of 'oops' and 'oow' rather than attempting to resurrect memories relative to occasions that may well be within memory.

This then is the side of the railway that was not intended to happen, but it did and will continue to do so. Today the stock involved may be different, the people wearing different fashions, and services restored by individuals who, seen by an alien from outer space, would believe to consist solely of orange skinned life forms.

If things ran perfectly this book could not exist, but from the interest the various accident reports that have occurred in 'Southern Way' plus the 'Wartime Southern' series have generated, it seems I am not alone at wanting to 'gawp'.

Kevin Robertson

editorial@thesouthernway.co.uk

ACKNOWLEDGEMENTS

I am indebted to a number of individuals and organisations who have yet again opened their files to assist in the compilation of this work. Foremost amongst these must be Bill Bishop who I first met in 1974 and who by then had already forgotten more about derailments on the Southern than I will ever know. It was Bill who also introduced me to Stephen Townroe, to both these men I owe a great deal - I only wish I had asked them more from their memory.

In more recent times a number of new friends have assisted. In alphabetical order these are, Mark Abbott, Eddie Barnes, Colin Boocock., Alan Butcher, Jeremy Cobb, David Flemings, Andy Gibbs / Pete Beyer, Tony Goodyear, Jeff Grayer / Ian Nolan, Tony Hillman, Gerald Jacobs, David Monk-Steel, Mike Morant, Viv Orchard and Dave Walden. To anyone else I may have omitted, my sincere apologies and a heartfelt thank-you. A special acknowledgement also to the wonderful Railway Accident Archive website.

Publishers Note

In life it is to be hoped we learn and evolve rather than continuously having to 'reinvent the wheel'. This very theme occurs in almost every book on accidents that has been produced, including this one, the same circumstances replicated due to a failure to learn from the lessons of the past. I will deliberately not cite examples, they will be immediately apparent in the following pages.

Where is this leading - simply this. A few years ago when we produced 'Wartime Southern' that series eventually grew to three volumes. Subject to the obvious business practicalities, we would like to continue with this series, so if you have Southern accident material of the type seen within these pages (cut off date around the mid to late 1970s) do please let us know.

ADDLESTONE - 5 August 1966

'D65xx' / Class '33'

The first of the illustrated incidents in this account of things that went awry is one on which we have little information other than the driver concerned admitted he had misjudged his braking distance. We know the date and the location, although a slightly more accurate description would be 'Addlestone - at the exit to the 'Up Siding West'. This as the name implies, was a siding, which also served Coxe's Mill - the company still receiving deliveries of grain by rail at this time. From personal knowledge, Tony Goodyear provides a account of the location and working of this siding, " The signal in the pictures is Addlestone's Down Home Signal No. 15 (easily recognisable as the main post is concrete, rare on the South Western), the loco derailed on the

trap end of No. 11 points, which was the exit from the Up Siding West, demolishing No. 12 shunt signal in the process. I remember it being out of use for a week or so. The grain wagons were usually propelled from the yard, wrong road, through 11 points reverse and then down the siding which was just short of a mile long (also used for recessing freight trains, when the need arose). At the mill end (inside the gate) there was a short loop holding about six wagons, these were then hauled in ones and twos under the unloading bay, using a capstan and rope. The grain was sucked out of the wagon and into a hopper, the empty wagons being returned to the other side of the loop to await collection."

Illustrations courtesy Andy Gibbs / Pete Beyer

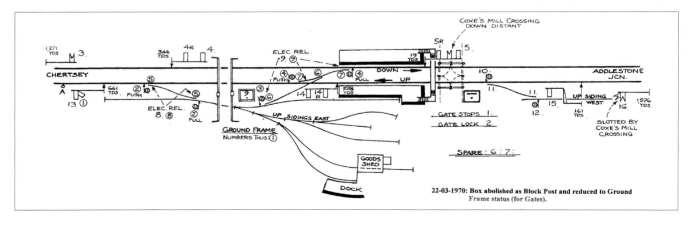

22-03-1970: Box abolished as Block Post and reduced to Ground Frame status (for Gates).

BARNES - 2 December 1955

Two x '2NOL' units, Nos. 1853 and 1877, also LMS '8F' 2-8-0
(the latter removed by the time the photographs were taken).

BARNES - 2 December 1955

The accident at Barnes was a sad case of signalman error - "irregular operation of the Sykes 'lock and block", was described by the inspecting officer. (Similar circumstances to that as occurred at St John's years before and which incident is described later.) At Barnes an electric train entered the section under clear signals and collided with the rear of a stationary freight, the force of the collision destroying the body of the guards van as well as a container ahead of it. The leading motor coach of the train (No. 9990 from set No. 1853) then fell over to the right and on to the adjacent down through line.

Again there were other factors that might be considered to have been minor contributory measures, but in the end the conclusions of Lieut. Col. G R S Wilson in a lengthy and thorough report were that the fault lay in the actions of either the signalman at Point Pleasant Junction or the man at Barnes Junction, the inspector concluding that the former was the most likely.

The Barnes accident occurred at approximately 11.28 pm, the weather not being a contributory factor on what was a fine clear night. Here we see the morning after the night before with debris being cleared and the riding vans of the Nine Elms breakdown crane alongside. Lieut. Col. Wilson was quick to point out that regardless of the culpability of the men involved, the initial outcome of the collision, whilst fatal for two railwaymen (the guard of the freight and motorman of the ELMU) , was not otherwise at first as serious as it became. Electrical arcing quickly caused a fire whilst the feeding of this of this fire by flammable materials contributed to make a bad situation far worse. Accordingly he had recommendations to make, not least with regard to the construction of the rolling stock involved, but countered this by stating the recent BR Modernisation plan had already dealt with the issue of a gradual replacement for wooden-bodied stock. The two electric sets concerned were introduced in 1935 and 1936 although in keeping with Southern Railway practice of the period, the coach bodywork was much older and had been originally constructed as loco-hauled stock between 1895 and 1900. Steel sheeting had been applied directly on to the wooden framework where the driving and electrical compartments were now located. The 'S15' opposite, No. 30500, was not involved and may well have arrived with an 'Officers Special' - could this even be how Lieut. Col. Wilson visited the scene - notice the head leaning out of the window of the coach.

The fire referred to completely burnt out the wooden bodywork of the first coach which was destroyed down to the underframe. The collision and fire accounted for 11 fatalities amongst the 30-40 passengers in the leading vehicle in addition to the two railwaymen referred to. A further 41 passengers were injured, 20 seriously.

Apart from the wooden body of the EMU providing fuel for the later inferno, it was found that paraffin oil and coal from the stove in the destroyed brake van were crucial in allowing the flames to gain a hold , whilst bitumen had recently been applied to the underside of the Queens Ride overbridge which spanned the tracks where the accident occurred. (Press reports refer to the

heat of the fire under the bridge being so intense that the structure buckled but this is not referred to in the official report.) They made a fateful combination, notwithstanding the prompt actions of both individuals and the fire brigade, indeed the flames were only just prevented from attacking the second coach of the front unit although some charring to the end did result.

The full report of the accident appears at http://www.railwaysarchive.co.uk/eventsummary.php?eventID=111 and need not be repeated here, although it should be mentioned that this report, in keeping with most formal accident reports, this report does not include illustrations within the text.

A similar - but not identical - view to that seen on page 8. In the foreground are the remains of the motor coach from the incinerated motor coach whilst just behind are burnt out vehicles from the freight train. The identity of the LMS '8F' was No. 48750, its crew also both suffered slight injuries, the driver who was sitting at the time of the collision having his head bruised whilst the fireman was 'stunned'. In the background a motor coach from an EMU is visible in the yard, probably the remaining part of the train involved shunted for inspection. Coach No 9990 was completely destroyed, its companion No. 9901 from Set No. 1853, was later broken up in the goods yard at Barnes.

BARNHAM - 1 August 1962

The dramatic scene shortly after the accident with passengers being helped from the compartments of the first carriage, this is where the more serious injuries were sustained. The smashed windows of the driving cab provided an escape route for the driver.

Three x '2BIL' units with No. 2088 leading

The Barnham accident, and for reasons which will be referred to later is perhaps even best described as an 'incident', was unusual in that it was caused by that most trivial of items - a metal washer - probably no more than 1 inch in diameter. The circumstances are recounted here by Jeffery Grayer drawing upon the recollections of Ian Nolan, a passenger on the train involved and who also took the photographs.

As the 10.17 am service to Portsmouth Harbour, consisting of three 2-coach sets of 2BIL electric stock, left Brighton station on the fine sunny morning of 1 August 1962, there was nothing untoward to alert the intending passenger that their journey was to be interrupted in spectacular fashion some 45 minutes later on the approach to Barnham station. The train was held at the home signal on the eastern approach to Barnham station for some two minutes whilst the previous service, the 9.18 am from Victoria, was dividing into separate Portsmouth and Bognor portions at the platform. With the platform clear the signalman lowered the home signal but did not take note of the point indicator above No. 8 lever for the simple reason these points had not been moved since the previous train had passed over them. The previously held EMU then proceeded into the station, at according to the driver "approximately 20 mph", but was immediately derailed at a set of partially open facing points on the approach and as a result was deflected on to the platform ramp. Here the first and second coaches overturned and although there were no serious injuries 37 passengers and the driver required hospital treatment.

In evidence given to the enquiry, the driver reported that as he approached the facing points he saw they were partially open and immediately closed the power controller and made an emergency brake application but this did not have time to take effect before the train was deflected towards the ramp of the platform. Immediately the front driving trailer ran up the platform and overturned to the right, to lie diagonally across both Down and Up lines. Fortunately the driver was unhurt and able to climb out of the broken front window. The front of the second coach followed the rear of the leading vehicle across to the Up line and it too was partly overturned to the right being supported by the platform. It was from this coach that our photographer made his lucky escape. These two coaches, forming the vehicles of set No. 2088, were extensively damaged both to the underframe and to the bogies and bodies, all four bogies coming away. The right side of the body of the leading coach and the roof were scored and distorted this caused by contact with the rails and the Up platform coping stones whilst the compartment partitions were separated from the floor. Luckily they did not collapse and most of the seat frames remained firm. The driving cab was pierced by two of the coping stones but fortunately the driver held his position on the left side of the cab and fell on top of the slab. The rear four coaches were not derailed and damage to them was slight. Following the accident both coaches of No. 2088 were written off.

The second carriage, in which Ian was travelling, lies propped against the platform edge allowing rescuers to access the compartments through the open doors, meanwhile passengers are being assisted from the track back up on to the platform.

17 year old Ian Nolan, who had joined the train at Hove, was a passenger in the second coach of the leading 2BIL unit No. 2088 of the train, he recalls that **" suddenly there was a change from running on rails to running on the platform**." Ian was on his way to the Railway Works Open Day at Eastleigh and fortunately had his camera with him. He had the presence of mind to take these images in the immediate aftermath recalling "...**any camera shake evident was probably due to having been in the tilted coach***!*" Fortunately none of the considerable trainload of 250 passengers sustained any serious injury and Ian was subsequently able to complete his journey to Eastleigh after changing on to buses provided to ferry passengers to Chichester where he then caught a train to Fratton changing into one bound for Eastleigh where he eventually arrived at 2.30 p.m.

Rescue and relief calls were promptly made and the response was excellent with Civil Defence and WVS personnel taking part in the rescue work ably assisted by workers from a nearby factory. West Sussex Fire and Rescue Service attended the scene. Approaching trains from Portsmouth and Bognor were halted at the respective home signals where passengers were de-trained and escorted to Barnham station. Littlehampton and Chichester became rail terminal points with emergency buses serving Bognor Regis en route. Goodwood race traffic was badly affected and in the evening a special was laid on from Chichester to Waterloo via Havant for returning race goers. At the time of the accident the

11:00 Brighton – Cardiff through train was into its journey and was diverted into Littlehampton where No. 34101 'Hartland' ran round its train and worked tender first up the mid Sussex line to Horsham at which point Ivatt tank No. 41327 coupled up to the rear and took the train to Guildford, via Baynards, and on to Woking where the SW mainline was rejoined for the trip to Salisbury and on to Cardiff. The 11:30 Brighton – Plymouth with No. 34012 'Launceston' in charge was diverted up the main London line to Redhill and ran via Guildford and Woking. In the reverse direction both Cardiff and Plymouth through trains ran via Woking and Redhill after parting from the Portsmouth sections at Salisbury. Arrival of the Cardiff service at Brighton, with N Class 31402 at the head from Redhill southwards, was a commendable 35 minutes late after this massive diversion. Both the Up and Down lines were restored to normal working in the early hours of the following day.

As it so often does, fate conspired to play a hand and approximately one minute before the accident occurred the rectifier in the Barnham sub-station went out of service and the circuit breakers between it and the d.c. traction bus bars opened. The third-rail power supply was then provided by adjacent sub-stations at Bognor, Ford and Drayton. The circuit breakers between the bus bars and the conductor rails at Barnham and at Yapton track paralleling hut opened for the Up and Down lines at 11:02, this automatic action being caused by the accident.

With the driver's comments about partially open

Above - Unit 2088 looking very much the worse for the experience with its bogies ripped off is surveyed by a couple of lady passengers no doubt contemplating their lucky escape. The damage to 2088 proved to be fatal and it was subsequently scrapped.

Right - Even though the EMU was only travelling at 20mph the smashed platform coping stones bear witness to the force of the impact.

facing points already known, a test later the same day by the S&T Inspector found that all circuits were in order but when he applied a volt meter across the reverse operating wire and the return wire for the facing points in question there was a large variation in voltage coinciding with the surge of power from the starting of trains from the loop line. As there should have been no voltage registering he undertook a careful examination of the circuit controller revealing an errant washer resting on the wiring underneath the controller bridging the reverse wire contact to a holding down screw on the frame of the controller. Upon removal of the washer no voltage was recorded.

The subsequent accident investigation undertaken by Colonel W P Reed confirmed that the facing points, which were motor worked, had been opened by the motor being incorrectly engaged; a loose washer having bridged the electrical circuit to enable this to happen. The diagram overleaf indicates the source of the problem but the Colonel was unable to conclude when the recalcitrant washer had been dropped and for how long it had lain innocently in the circuit controller. Whilst allowing that during routine maintenance a washer might drop unnoticed and therefore not be searched for, he nevertheless stressed that this should not have happened and stated that appropriate instructions be issued in the S&T Department to emphasize the consequences that can arise from the smallest mistake in signal equipment maintenance.

The S&T Department admitted that there had been instances of faulty operation of motor-worked points elsewhere on BR through false feeds and it had been recognised that it was desirable to provide a contact normally open in the negative lead from the points motor as well as the operating contacts for reverse and normal in the positive leads which would only be closed by the lever operating the points. Such an arrangement would have prevented the faulty operation of points in the Barnham incident. There was a programme on the SR to make this alteration at 337 sets of

motor-worked points but so far only about half had so far been dealt with. The Colonel recorded, in conclusion, that the remainder of the work had now been afforded a higher priority and that all such points should have this additional protection within the next 6-12 months.

Jeffery Grayer also recalls, "I remember seeing a report in my local newspaper, the Chichester Observer, about a railway accident just one stop up the line from my home station."

Ian returned home later in the day from Eastleigh to Fratton where he boarded a train for Chichester changing there for a bus to Littlehampton via Barnham. He then caught a Victoria bound train from Littlehampton back to Hove where he arrived with quite a story to tell his parents. He was none the worse for his adventure however, and did not let his experience on that day deter him from a lifelong interest in railways.

Looking east from Barnham's island platform the scale of the disruption to services is evident with both Up and Down lines, in addition to the Bognor Regis bay on the right, being well and truly blocked.

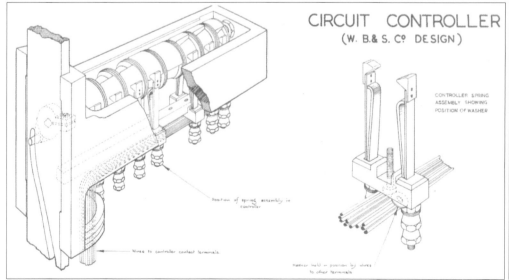
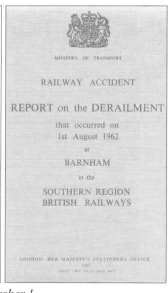

Diagram of circuit controller taken from the Accident Report showing the position of that washer !

Top - *Looking east, the first pair of coaches lie amongst the tangled mass of debris. Unit 2088 had been in the wars previously and was actually a hybrid being former of a BIL motor coach and a HAL trailer from unit No. 2653, the original trailer having been destroyed by fire in 1950. In 1951 units 2088 and 2029 permanently exchanged driving trailers.*

Bottom - *Taken from the Up platform looking west this view shows a railway official surveying the damage to the second and third coaches of the train. Damage to the second BIL unit was slight and it was subsequently repaired and put back into service.*

BERMONDSEY - 19 December 1899

Accidents before Christmas always seem to strike a particular chord, such as the rear-end collision near Bermondsey intermediate signal box on morning of 19 December 1899.

About 8.17 am, the 8.07 am London Bridge to Victoria train was waiting at the down starting signal of the signal box referred to when it was run into at low speed by the following 8.10 am, London Bridge to Oxted service. Two passengers were killed, four railway staff severely injured (three had been travelling as passengers in the Victoria train) and about 12 other passengers complained of injuries. Stock wise the damage was light, as might be expected it was limited to the rear vehicle of the Victoria train - a brake van - and the engine of the Oxted working, 'D3' 0-4-4T No. 388.

Bermondsey intermediate signal box was in effect no more than a break-section signal box on what was an extremely busy section of line, indeed there were nine sets of rails in front of it, although only one, the LBSCR down south-London line is relevant.

On the day in question it was foggy. There are conflicting accounts as to the severity of the fog; and to be fair fog can on occasions vary in density very rapidly. Fog-men were not on duty at the time of the accident although the driver of both the Victoria service and the driver of the offending train felt they should have been.

The Victoria train had been brought to a halt at the Bermondsey Intermediate starting signal for the simple reason that the section ahead was blocked. It was, or should have been, perfectly safe in that it was protected in rear by the home signal for Bermondsey Intermediate, and second advanced starting signal at South London signal box, both of these showing 'Danger'. Due to the short block sections the distant signal for the former signal was on the same post as the latter and this too was showing 'on'. 'Sykes lock and block' was in use on this line and was being worked correctly, certainly not an occasion where irregular use of the release key applied - a feature of more than one accident in subsequent pages.

The driver of No. 388 was Edward Herriett. He had 26 years experience working for the LBSCR, 21 years as a driver. Herriett had arrived for a 12-hour shift at 6.30 am, having previously finished work at 4.10 pm the previous day, he admitted he knew the road well. Leaving from Platform 5 at London Bridge at 8.10 am, Herriett stated he had a clear view of the first three stop signals which were all off, but then came the crucial words, "....the next signal was the London Bridge south advanced started; *this signal I took to be off*. From what the signalman subsequently told me I know that it could not have been off. My explanation of thinking that it was off is, that on account of the fog I could only just see it, and I distinctly took it to be off. I looked at it very carefully as I passed it, and distinctly thought it was off." Herriett was driving slowly, 5 mph or so, and whilst he did not see the indication of the stop signal he admitted the distant which was on the same post was certainly 'on' The distant was

warning the indication of the following stop signal but here fate takes a hand as Herriett missed this next stop signal completely. He continues "...on account of the fog I could not see it at all so I ran past it, not knowing whether it was on or off but I did not know I was past until I saw the box." By this time speed was about 10 mph, whilst having realised his error at misjudging his exact position he shut off steam and looked ahead - it was only then he saw the stationary train, about 15 yards, in front. The brakes were applied but the dampness created by the fog meant the rails were greasy and there was little appreciable reduction in speed before the actual impact. Herriett commented he was surprised over the lack of fog-men. He admitted he was aware of the rules about proceeding with caution in such conditions and agreed that even 10 mph was probably too fast under the circumstances. Fireman Hartfield corroborated his driver's remarks as to the poor visibility, stating that he been engaged in firing when they must have passed the respective signals but that also the fog was so thick, "...you could not properly see a signal more than 20 yards away from you."

We are not informed of Herriett's fate, caution, demotion, dismissal, all were the sanctions a man might expect under the circumstances. Herriett's explanation is included as it would otherwise be all too easy to consider one viewpoint alone. The fact that he was in charge of the train cannot mean any subsequent mitigation may absolve him of the final responsibility, but as in other formal accident reports, there do remain unanswered questions, principal of these being why were fog-men not on duty, what were the criteria applicable before they might be called out and was there even some pressure on the signalmen involved to attempt to avoid their use?

Whilst it was not possible to pluck a man off the street and give him 26 years railway experience overnight, there were still plenty of men ready to jump into a railway career if a sudden vacancy at the top meant everyone else was suddenly shuffled forward. For the railway companies labour was both cheap and plentiful.

Putting aside the issue of cost that may have been a factor in calling out fog-men, the other factor here was the way such an accident might have been prevented had a form of ATC/AWS been available. Just a few years later in 1906 the GWR would pioneer their ATC system where an indication was available to the driver as to the position of the distant signal. Elsewhere the failsafe track-circuit had already been introduced by the American engineer William Robinson in 1872, whilst in 1901 the 'trip-cock' would also be pioneered in America. It would be many years before use of these various safety devices became commonplace, whilst their potential in the prevention of accidents and therefore the saving of lives would be commented upon by inspecting officers with both increasing frequency and vigour at the time of numerous future investigations.

Meanwhile Herriett alone was the subject of the damning last sentence of Lieut. Col P G von Donop's report, "Whilst therefore, it appears most probable that with due care driver Herriett could have seen that the signals were against him, even if that was not the case, proper caution on his part should have prevented the collision occurring. The whole responsibility for the accident must, therefore, rest on his shoulders, and no other servant of the Company appears to be in any way to blame."

'D3' No. 388

No. 388, minus chimney, following the collision. From the debris nearby it would appear the damaged stock was re-located to a nearby yard. The engine was repaired and ran until 1951.

'Hastings' DEMU, 2 separate 4-Car BR EMU sets.

Borough Market Junction on 28 January 1960 was fortunate to have been a low-speed accident. Even so at what is regarded as one of the Southern Region 'mission critical' locations the knock-on effects were considerable so far as other traffic was concerned. The facts though are simply told.

At 2.58 pm the 1.00pm DEMU from Hastings to Charing Cross was running through London Bridge and Borough Market Junction on its way to Charing Cross. The train was proceeding on the up local line under clear signals with two qualified drivers in the cab. Borough Market Junction is the point of convergence of the up through and up local lines, the stop signal at the end of the up through line showing a red aspect. Approaching this signal was the 2.22 pm electric service from Hayes to Charing Cross. This train had stopped at London Bridge and then left on the up through line when the starting signal showed 'off'. It should however have only pulled up as far as the junction signal but instead the driver continued forward so coming into a side-long collision with the Hastings train. The impact severely damaged the front motor coach of DEMU set (no set or vehicle numbers for any of the trains involved are reported) in addition to causing similar damage to the front two coaches of the Hayes train. These three vehicles were derailed. Unfortunately the impact caused the rear end of the front motor coach from the EMU to be pushed into the path of the down line from Charing Cross and here it was struck almost at once by the lead vehicle of the 2.53 pm Charing Cross to Tattenham Corner service. In total there were some 238 passengers on board the three trains, seven of whom, mostly in the Hayes train, were slightly injured. Only one was treated in hospital and this person was discharged shortly afterwards.

Clearing the line and restoration of damage to track and signal was achieved in just over 14 hours, ready for the rush-hour on the following day. The driver of the offending train, that from Hayes, was adamant his own junction signal had been clear for him to proceed but exhaustive tests failed to corroborate his recollections whilst the signalmen concerned were similarly adamant they had not altered the routes set as either train approached. Seen above the two men may well be press photographers, both of whom appear to have little regard for their own safety.

Left - *From what is a poor quality view, the identification of the Hayes set may well be that of S5360 but this cannot be confirmed. The front of the Tattenham Corner train which ran into the collision can also be seen in the background.*

Bottom - *The sideswiped front coach from the Hayes train after the Tattenham service had been removed. It can only be imagined the forces involved to create this type of damage consequently it was indeed fortunate there were so few injuries and that the whole episode occurred at slow speed.*

Right - A second roof view, taken by one of those seen earlier perhaps? A contemporary report differed slightly from the official wording in that it stated 11 persons had been injured.

Bottom - From the opposite side of the line, the impact damage to the front coach of the Hayes train is clear, the front vehicle from this likely to be overhanging the bridge. Over-runs (or what are nowadays referred to as 'S.P.A.Ds' become critical in places such as the congested layout at Borough Market where it is not always possible to provide the normal 440 yard clearing point. Fortunately in such locations speeds are invariably low.

BR 'Standard Class 4' No. 76017

Events such as those seen on this and that seen overleaf were rarely reported outside of railway circles. It was very much a question of restore the traffic situation as soon as possible and enquire afterwards - a total opposite to the criteria that applies today (as is recounted in the introduction). Consequently the derailment of No. 76017 has only reached the history books as the witness was not only an enthusiast but also a professional railwayman!

The engine has managed to split the points on the single exit road out of the depot at Bournemouth Central on 29 June 1958. Re-railing ramps are in position in the hope that the engine can be driven back the way it came and so re-rail itself on the way. (The outcome was not reported, but until the recalcitrant machine can be moved the depot was effectively 'shut'.) Meanwhile the fireman carries on arranging the coal in the tender, oblivious to the injector that has blown off! (There was always plenty of advice standing around at these events!)

No. 76017 was no stranger to finding itself other than where it was intended to be, for this was the same engine involved in the derailment at Whitchurch Town (DNS line) on 23 September 1954 when it ran away, being unable to stop at the end of the down loop. Bournemouth Central too had witnessed a serious collision three years earlier in 1955 involving two steam engines meeting almost head-on near the same point. This last is described in Issue No 13 of *'The Southern Way'*

Image and information courtesy of Colin Boocock

BOURNEMOUTH CENTRAL - 2 December 1961

'West Country' No. 34045

On Saturday 2 December 1961, No 34045 'Ottery St. Mary' ran through the trap points at the end of the down platform at Bournemouth Central and demolished the buffer stops, fortunately coming to rest before reaching the abutment of Beechey Road bridge. The breakdown gang is busy with cutting gear disentangling the West Country from the mangled wreckage of the buffer stops.

Image and information courtesy of Colin Boocock

BOURNEMOUTH WEST - 17 August 1956

Runaway coaches

Severe damage to the station awning and the parcels office at Bournemouth West was caused on 17 August 1956 by the stock of the 11.16 am Newcastle train which ran away down the 1 in 68 gradient from the carriage sidings out of control and without a locomotive attached. Quick thinking by the signalman diverted the vehicles into the siding adjoining No. 6 platform, where there was a violent collision with a train of three coaches and van standing. The force of the impact meant the standing stock was driven through the buffer stops and severely damaged. Not surprisingly these coaches intended for the Newcastle train could now not be used and so an assortment of vehicles was put together although lacking the usual restaurant car. Seen the next morning, the coaches have been moved and the debris is in the process of being cleared, the van on the left had been placed in position to act as a temporary buffer stop. (See also notes from personal observation by Mike Morant overleaf.)

Colin Boocock

THE OTHER SIDE OF THE SOUTHERN

From personal observation by Mike Morant

"On Friday 17 August 1956 a train spotter aged 13 and his nine years old younger brother were standing at the country end of platform 4 at Bournemouth West station whiling away the time whilst their parents went into the town centre to do some shopping. Not much used to happen at that station other than on summer Saturdays but this was to change dramatically on that Friday morning.

"It was normal to see coaching stock movements descending the steep slope from the sidings into the station with apparently no engine attached, as had been done at Bournemouth West on countless occasions since the year dot and with the usual sound operating reasons. [1]

"On this occasion there appeared to be something amiss as the stock in question was a lengthy train that seemed to be heading for platform 6 - in which a train already stood - whilst the stock that was moving appeared to be gathering pace rather than slowing - as would normally be the case.

"The spotters' fears were justified as they saw the thirteen coach set, intended for the 11.16 a.m. York/ Newcastle train, hurtle into platform 6 followed swiftly by a massive thud that shook the ground under their feet [2] as the out of control stock ploughed into the three coaches plus a van that intended to form the 11.34 to Southampton Central. The resultant cloud of dust took a long time to settle and the spotters then made their way to the town end of the station where they were confronted with the scene depicted above.

"The damage to the end of the station building was extensive but what was remarkable was that, as they later found out, nobody had been killed or seriously maimed, which explains why the subsequent enquiry was purely an internal one and didn't involve the government appointed inspectorate of the day. There was, however, some damage on the station's forecourt, to two cars, one of which was cloven in two immediately behind the bonnet (see opposite). The contemporary report in the *Bournemouth Echo* newspaper on the day of the accident also reported that the parcels office was demolished and one woman had been slightly injured.

"But what had actually happened? There have been variations on this tale over the years but it is probable that the definitive one is now at hand thanks to contemporaneous local railway knowledge. Peter Smith ('Mendips Engineman') who worked for BR locally at that time, recalls that the stock that ran away had earlier been attended to by fitters in the sidings that morning and that they had probably forgotten to apply the brakes after finishing their work. The locomotive designated as the stock's 'pusher' down to the station area simply followed the normal procedure by buffering up, but that was sufficient to set the rake moving with no possibility of it being halted in a controlled way. With commendable speed, phone calls to the signalman had the train routed to

No. 6 Platform where it would, hopefully, cause the least damage and that appears to have been the right decision.

"The wrecked Maunsell coach shown above is No. 3783 which formed part of three coach set No. 330 but at the time of writing the identity of the van which was also destroyed in the crash is not known. It was probably down to the quick thinking of the signalman that there was also nobody present in the parcels office when the accident occurred."

Note 1: These notes were compiled in July/August 2011 when there had been a recent exchange of messages within the SEmG message board environment regarding whether or not fly shunting of stock from the West carriage sidings down to the station's buffers still occurred in 1956. The consensus was that the practice had been banned many years before that but this writer believes that it was still commonplace for short trains - such as the stock for the 11.34 to Southampton Central.

Note 2: Peter Smith recalls that he, like the spotters' parents, was shopping in the centre of Bournemouth at the time of the accident, he heard the sound of the collision even from that distance.

Sources: Brian MacDermott without whose persistence this heavily revised article wouldn't have been written and also for his supply of notes, research and images relating to this incident which have been priceless.
Peter Smith for his contemporary local knowledge and research into historical resources.
Maunsell's SR Steam Passenger Stock 1923-1939, by David Gould. Published by Oakwood Press, 1978.
Maunsell's SR Steam Carriage Stock by David Gould. Published by Oakwood Press, third printing 2000, ISBN 0 85361 555 1

Over a week later the incident was still making news locally, as witness the 'Bournemouth Echo' of 25 August 1956.

"Six buffer incidents at Bournemouth West Station in 10 years - Transport Commission's reply to 'What again', query.

"Since the Bournemouth West station mishap on August 17 when part of the roof was demolished, local people have been asking one other, 'How many times has a similar incident occurred?'

"As news of the crash spread around the town, public reaction was 'What again?' In view of this feeling, and correspondence received on the matter, the 'Echo' took up the matter with the British Transport Commission. It was on these lines that the 'Echo' based their investigation.

"Regarding the first question, the BTC replied that since 1946 and prior to the mishap in August 17 only six accidents involving stock coming into contact with buffer stops occurred at the station. Five cases were due to 'failure of the human element' and one to defective gear. In no case did serious injury result, either to passengers or staff.

RECOMMENDATIONS ADOPTED

"At the inquiries into these mishaps, the following recommendations were made: (1) In 1948 that the weight of trains being shunted should be reduced from 12 to 6 coaches when gravitated, and (2) In 1949, that gravitation shunting should be prohibited altogether. Both these recommendations were adopted. *(Were they...?)*

"This supports the theory expressed by Echo reporters - who were on the scene shortly after last week's accident - that the runaway coaches could have been accidentally 'nudged' into motion by a train in the passenger siding.

"In fairness to the Commission it must be admitted that in view of the traffic using West station, six mishaps in a decade is not a high rate. No less than 58 loaded and empty trains arrive and 54 loaded and empty trains depart every day Monday to Friday, during the summer period. On Saturdays these figures are increased to 63 and 64 respectively.

"Says a BTC spokesman: 'Safety is regarded as of the utmost importance by British Railways, and practical measures are taken to assist wherever possible in combatting failures, whether technical or human, and which unfortunately occur from time to time.

"The Commission's reply is in no way connected with the inquiry held this week into the causes of the crash, when 13 runaway coaches rammed stationary stock in a siding. A spokesman at Waterloo told me the findings of this enquiry will not be made public. 'There are two types of enquiry held by the BTC', he said. 'If public property is damaged or injury sustained, then the enquiry is of a public nature. If only railway property is involved, then a domestic enquiry is held and the result is not published.'

WON'T BE TOLD

"So we shall not know what caused the mishap, although on this occasion it could be suggested that the enquiry might have been public - two private cars were wrecked by the crashing station roof, and one woman slightly injured. *(Surely this WAS an incident where the findings might be made public.)*

"One letter on the subject comes from Mr E G F Pittar of Poole who at first refers generally to railway accidents but then pertinently asks, 'We know that the duties of railwaymen are many and arduous, but would it not be in the public interest if the blame - if blame there is - could be fairly apportioned between the men, the management, and circumstances beyond the control of either?'

THREE QUESTIONS ASKED

"The recent smash-up at Bournemouth West station, which could have been so serious in injury and loss of life, might serve to pinpoint one aspect of the problem near at home. Mr Pittar then asks three questions, the first having been broached by many: 'How many accidents have occurred at West Station involving stock over-running the stops? What safety measures, if any, have been recommended as a result of enquiries into such accidents? Have these recommendations been adopted?"

BURNING BULLEIDS

The consequence of the pyrotechnics which affected No. 34057 'Biggin Hill' at Hamble Halt on 22 May 1961 feature on the front cover of this book - similarly a set of three b/w images of the same occurrence plus a detailed explanation appear in Issue No 4 of 'The Southern Way' - the full circumstances of this incident need not then be repeated. Suffice to say the accompanying colour views, unavailable when Issue No. 4 was being prepared, depict the whole episode in a new light. In the top view fire brigade personnel and railwaymen are still present whilst clearly the incident was a spectacle worth watching by members of the public from the opposite side of the line. Meanwhile No. 76066 passes by with an ordinary service train bound for

Fareham, having been 'cautioned' past the scene. In the centre view, on the left No. 76019 has arrived 'wrong line' to rescue the ensemble. Locomotive and train were then pulled forward to the next station at Netley where (lower view) the 'still simmering' No. 34057 was placed in a siding at the east end of the station. (The LSWR lower quadrant signal was the home signal for the former Hospital branch.) No. 34057 was subsequently removed to Eastleigh under tow from a BR Class 4 2-6-4T.

This page, all - Roger Holmes

Opposite page - No. 34020, formerly 'Seaton' - but seen here devoid of name and numberplates - 'dumped' at Exmouth Junction with the effects of a casing fire only too visible. This was the final depot for this engine from where it was withdrawn in May 1964, possibly as a result of what is seen here. (No. 34020 will be seen again later in consequence of an incident that occurred at St. Denys.)

John Morgan

Two more examples of fires on Bulleid pacifics. Above No. 21C2 'Union Castle' displays a limited amount of heat damage, but compared with below - No. 21C119 'Bideford' has clearly been the subject of heat of a far greater intensity. What makes this image so interesting is that at the time the engine was the sole member of the Bulleid type to have been converted to burn oil, hence the tank top seen on the tender. The view was recorded at Eastleigh by S C Townroe around May 1948, although details of where and when the actual fire occurred are not reported. Without further information it would be unfair to apportion blame, although it must be said that most engines that were converted to burn oil around this time and regardless of class, could suffer the effects of leaking oil igniting in the ashpan. Possibly the latter was a contributory factor.

COCKING - 19 November 1951

'C2X' No. 32552

In November 1951, heavy rain caused localized flooding which in turn blocked a culvert resulting in a breach of the embankment on the single line between Cocking and Midhurst (close to the present day Holmbush Industrial Estate). On 19 November, the daily pick up goods departed from Chichester for Midhurst as normal, stopping first at Lavant and then Singleton to put off and collect traffic.

Then came the run to Midhurst, the latter station approached on a falling gradient and curve. At this point the fireman, George Howes was looking out of the driver's side of the engine cab, commenting later that he had never seen so much water on both sides of the line. Looking ahead there was at first nothing untoward - indeed their next destination at Midhurst could be viewed through the trees, but suddenly George noticed the tracks ahead were unsupported, the force of water against the blocked culvert had washed away the associated embankment leaving the rails with nothing underneath and dangling in mid air. Both George and his driver Fred Bunker jumped from the footplate, George managed to land on level ground but Fred had slipped down the bank and was initially up to his knees in water.

Meanwhile their engine, 'C2X' No. 32522 forged ahead, that is until its weight caused the unsupported rails to collapse beneath. At this point it fell into the gap

coming to an abrupt halt but with the tender forced upright and the wagons from the train piled beneath. Both loco-men were uninjured, mainly due to the following wagons not falling on to the side of the line where they had landed. The resultant tender full of coal plus a wagon load of anthracite immediately behind the locomotive subsequently caused a fire which burnt for some time. The guard was also able to jump clear.

The telegraph wires and pole route had been unaffected, hence there had been no advance warning which might otherwise only have been noted upon the next walking inspection by the ganger.

With the engine partly submerged and the firebox crown uncovered due to the angle at which it was resting, there was some concern over an explosion. Help was summoned by telephone from a nearby pub on the public road alongside, although not before complaints had been received from two ladies over the noise and escaping steam which hung around the ground on what was already a damp, foggy autumnal day.

Because of this perceived risk of explosion, the fire brigade and an ambulance attended although eventually the boiler was deemed safe with the fire both in the firebox and within the vicinity of the engine cab, allowed to burn itself out. (Hence the scorched appearance of the cab as seen in the images.)

Recovery of No.32552 was effected in a similar way to that undertaken at Hither Green and Shawford - both described later. A crane was brought in as close as possible to the site which was then used to remove the damaged wagons and tender, the engine itself being unable to be lifted by the crane due to the soft ground.

Consequently the next stage was to cut away the embankment whilst also packing the engine underneath as much as possible to prevent it sinking further. Some dismantling of the motion also took place. The illustrations of the conditions indicate that this is in itself was no easy task. After track was laid the locomotive was winched back using Kelbus gear in the direction of Chichester.

At the time the engine was already nearly 50 years old and so it must be asked if consideration was even given to dismantling it on the spot - as had happened at Waterloo when an 'M7' fell down the shaft of the 'Waterloo & City' and as also took place at Shapwick (S&D) in 1949.

In the event No. 32552 was repaired and remained in service until 1961 although no such repairs were made to the culvert. Thus the Chichester - Midhurst line, which according to S C Townroe writing in 1953, "...was scheduled for closure in the near future anyway", ceased to exist as a through route from that time on. To be fair it was already just used for freight and from that time on until complete closure, was operated as what was in effect a dead-end siding from Chichester.

Images S C Townroe / R Blencowe collection (3) M Morant (1)

Left - Two weeks on and viewed from the Midhurst side of the now severed railway, No 32552 awaits recovery.
2 December 1951.
J J Smith / Bluebell Railway Archive

DEVON BELLE INCIDENT- 22 September 1947

On 22 September 1947 an unusual incident befell the engine of the Up 'Devon Belle' as the train was travelling between Sidmouth Junction and Honiton. At that point the service passed the down 'Atlantic Coast Express' whereupon the offside wingplate proclaiming 'Devon Belle' became detached. Unfortunately the broken plate proceeded to cut into the cowling of the engine of the 'ACE' whilst jagged lumps smashed windows in both trains injuring seven passengers. Notwithstanding the passenger injuries no formal accident report has been found. Seen here workmen are attaching (detaching) a wingplate on another occasion - probably at Nine Elms. We know at least one photograph of the culprit locomotive with the wingplate twisted round exists - it was seen in an album of photographs for sale some years ago. Regretfully this was before 'SW' had been commenced, but if the current owner were to read this..! S C Townroe / R Blencowe collection

EASTLEIGH - 8 February 1955

'H15' No. 30477

On 8 February 1955, 'H15' 4-6-0 No. 30477 ran through the trap points at the exit from Eastleigh depot and ended up in the dirt, thankfully clear of the main line. The Eastleigh 35-ton breakdown crane was tackling the job of righting the engine when photographed late in the evening.   Colin Boocock

EASTLEIGH - 23 January 1959

Mineral wagon

A 16ton mineral wagon came off at the points at the "top end" of Eastleigh East Yard on 23 January 1959. Because it was nearby, the Eastleigh steam crane was used to put the wagon back on the rails. A definite case of a "sledge-hammer to crack a nut" indeed!

Colin Boocock

FARNBOROUGH - FLEET 4 November 1926

The four track section of main line between Farnborough and Fleet was the location of a rear-end collision between a passenger train and an empty milk train early on the morning of 4 November 1926.

Stationary, on the down through line about 6.39 am, but under the protection of fixed signals in the rear, was the 4.15 am Victoria to Yeovil empty milk churn train, comprising locomotive No. E775 behind which were eleven 4-wheel vehicles (vans, carriage trucks or milk vans), five 6-wheel vehicles and three 8-wheel brake-vans. Driver Meaton on No. E775 had received a distant signal at 'on' as he passed Farnborough and so reduced the speed of the train. When approaching the relevant stop signal he saw from a distance of about 100 yards this too was at danger and so applied the brake more fully. The train was 'fully fitted' and consequently the brakes would have been applied throughout the train, but almost as soon as the brakes had been applied the stop signal changed to 'off' whereupon the driver released the brake and applied steam. Unfortunately this braking and then accelerating caused a snatch, resulting in the train parting after the fifth vehicle, both sections coming to rest quickly and at this stage without incident. It was now about 6.31 am. (Subsequent analysis of the failed coupling revealed a long-standing flaw which, it was considered, would have been visually difficult to detect.)

Both portions of the divided train were ahead of the stop signal, the signals on this section being of the low-pressure pneumatic type and although there were track-circuits to the rear of the signal there were none in advance of the signal. The stationary milk service was standing with its rear some 131 yards ahead of the protecting signal.

A consultation then took place between the guard and driver, whereupon it was decided that the driver would set back under the a Guard's 'Wrong Line Order'. This was achieved quickly, but whilst it was a straightforward task to re-establish the coupling, the vacuum pipe was more difficult, due it was said, to the earlier separation of the train. Consequently it was necessary for the driver to return to his engine for a hammer in an attempt to rectify matters.

All this time No. E772 at its two-part train was stationary on the main line and at no time had the guard considered it necessary to walk back the few yards to the signal bridge behind him from which the rules stated he should immediately telephone the signalman in the event of such an occasion arising. This was in addition to the normal requirement of placing detonators to protect the rear. It appears the re-coupling had almost been completed with both driver and guard between the vehicles concerned when they were alerted to the sound of an approaching train. Realising it was likely to be coming up behind them, both men quickly managed to extricate themselves just as No. E452 at the head of the 5.40 am Waterloo to Bournemouth and Weymouth collided at speed with the rear of their stationary milk train.

The force of the impact turned No. E452 over to its right side continuing this way before coming to rest some 120 yards west fouling the up main line. Behind No

'King Arthur' No. E452

34

Senior officers inspect the damage. The three coaches immediately behind the engine were Nos. 3222, 5143 and 3233. Not surprisingly it was reported there was considerable damage to the permanent way and, it was reported, signalling. Presumably the latter would be a reference to electrical and / or pneumatic equipment.

E452 were 12 vehicles, of mixed 8, 6 and 4-wheel type, the first three being bogie coaches. Of these the two at the front were derailed as was the front bogie of vehicle number three. All three coaches were forced across into the space between the fast lines but did not overturn. There was no telescoping.

Not so the vehicles from the milk train. Here the force of the impact, estimated to have been at least 40mph, totally destroyed the ten rearmost vehicles whilst in addition the remaining stock and the train engine, meaning No E772, were pushed forward some 20 yards. All four lines were now obstructed although the actions of the guards of both trains with detonators prevented any further incident occurring.

Considering the speed involved casualties were remarkably light, the worse affected being the driver of the passenger train who was badly burned and succumbed to his injuries a few days later. The fireman of this train was also injured, as were two passengers (out of about 15-16 travelling) and three Post Office sorters - vehicle No 8 was a 6-wheel TPO van.

The enquiry centred upon two facts, firstly why had the driver of the passenger train failed to respond to the indications given by the preceding signals and why had the guard of the failed train not taken the required action to protect his train?

In the first instance the evidence of the fireman was crucial. This man, stated the fireman, had always struck him as responsible in his actions for with steam beating down on both sides of the engine in addition to a low mist, he had noticed the driver crossing the footplate on a number of occasions in order to obtain the best view ahead – *see note about the position of the signals on these gantries in the lower caption opposite*. The fireman had not seen the position of the signals previous to the collision and the first he knew was when the driver suddenly shut the regulator and made a full brake application. He estimated they were travelling about at 50 mph at this time.

No doubt was cast upon the operation of the signals nor that the light illuminating the lens of the spectacle glass was operating. The rear light of the standing train was also lit.

Why the deceased driver failed to act will never be known, possibly he simply missed the crucial indication of the preceding distant signal, we will just never know. What this accident did of course throw into question was the lack of a track circuit in advance of each stop signal, but it would be some years before such matters were dealt with. Until then the anomaly would exist, there was in effect no 'clearing point' should a train fail to stop and such action would not be known about as

the location of many of the signals on this section was in open country.

Colonel Pringle recommended 'Automatic Train Control', and whilst also acknowledging that the deceased driver must take primary responsibility the inaction of the guard of the milk train was justifiably, also criticised.

To clear the scene, steam cranes from Nine Elms, Guildford and Salisbury were requisitioned, the up local line being cleared at 8.0am. The passengers from the 5.40am train were detrained and walked to Fleet station, whence they continued their journey by a local service, which was arranged between Fleet and Basingstoke. The down local line between Farnborough and Fleet was cleared at 11.54pm on the 4th November, and the down and up through lines at 3.50am on the 5th November. Single line working was in force over the up local line during the period of obstruction and arrangements were made for as many trains as possible to be worked via Alton, including the majority of the Bournemouth trains.

Left - Debris from some of the ten destroyed vehicles of the milk train litter the tracks. Engine No. E452 was just 18 months old at the time of accident, it was repaired and lasted in service well into BR days. Ironically it would be involved in a further rear-end collision on the same piece of line years later. This was just east of Woking on 10 November 1945 when the renumbered No. 452 ran into the rear of a slow-moving passenger train ahead. There were no fatalities but several persons were injured.

Above - An unusual, for the time, arial view of the crash site. By the time the engine of the offending passenger service had come to rest, the signal to the rear of the train was some little way off to the right and therefore out of camera. Near to the scene was Bramshot Halt, the green-keeper from the nearby Bramshot golf club had been standing at the entrance to the down platform and witnessed the collision. He confirmed he had heard the passenger train approaching but was unable to see the signals owing to the mist. Former railwayman Gerald Jacobs raises an interesting point over the positioning of the automatic signals on their respective gantries on this section of line which stood centrally above the actual rails. Gerald's comments, "Adams built his engines with right hand drive; Drummond on the left. Was the position of the signals in the centre a compromise? This was a real factor in the St. John's disaster of 1957. In foggy weather proceeding at caution was the order of the day between Woking and Basingstoke hence it was vital the guard should have complied with Rule 227 on the detonators alone, had he done so there is a reasonable chance the passenger train may have been able to stop."

All photographs courtesy Jeremy Cobb

FOREST ROW - 3 March 1954

'K' No. 32346

On 3 March 1954 No. 32346 ran out of control descending Brambletye bank at the head of a Three Bridges to Buxted engineer's train. The engine was derailed at the end of the sand drag at Forest Row station and fell on its side into soft ground part way down a shallow embankment. The running lines were cleared overnight, leaving the engine, tender, plus a damaged brake-van to be recovered later. Meanwhile regular services, passenger and freight, were resumed with passengers treated to the embarrassing (for British Railways that is) spectacle of one aspect of train working the authorities would rather not have been seen. It is interesting to note no attempt was made to cover or shield the offending engine from view.

Recovery was achieved four days later on Sunday 7 March, the sight of two separate breakdown trains with their respective cranes was probably the greatest concentration of the traffic the station had witnessed for some time.

On what was a dull, wet March day, No. 32346 was hoisted from its resting place and returned to the rails, the tender having been dealt with beforehand. Notwithstanding the weather, it was clearly an occasion considered worth watching by the assembled spectators. After inspection, the engine was cleared to be towed to Brighton for repair. It remained in traffic until 1962. The following day, 8 March 1954, a operational test run was made by the Motive Power department involving a train of similar weight and composition from Three Bridges to Groombridge via Forest Row and return. An engine of the same class, No. 32351 was used. The descent of the bank into Forest Row was successfully achieved, although it was admitted this was in better weather conditions than had been experienced by No. 32346. On the return the bank had to be climbed, which, according to a correspondent in the 'Railway Observer' "...was something memorable to both see and hear with such a heavy load."

All illustrations J J Smith / Bluebell Railway Archive

GOMSHALL - 20 February 1904

The accident at Gomshall on 20 February 1904 was a simple case of too high a speed for the prevailing conditions - ironically echoing some of the circumstances of Sevenoaks 20 plus years later.

'O' class 0-6-0 No. 284 was approaching Gomshall station with a train of seven vehicles: a 4-wheel brake van, followed by six 6-wheel coaches and the last a third-class brake. The working was a military special from Gravesend bound for Southampton. No set time was shown for passing Gomshall, although the train was noted to have passed Dorking at 10.15 am running about three minutes early - having also left Redhill three minutes early.

According to the driver of the train, No. 284 entered Gomshall about 35 mph, a speed confirmed by the guard, and the Gomshall signalman, although two other men, a relief signalman working nearby and a goods checker felt the speed to have been nearer 40 mph - consider though that at the time there were no such things as speedometers and opinions could vary. The local ganger was also nearby as the train passed and he placed the speed around 50 mph with 'steam still on'. Whatever, as the engine approached the trailing crossover at the end of the station the leading wheels left the rails with the train following. The drag beam between the locomotive and tender also parted so engine and tender finished up facing in opposite directions

Considerable damage was caused to the permanent way whilst it was admitted the crossover in question was noted as being of the 'old' type and according to Mr Tempest, the Chief Engineer of the SECR, only suitable for a maximum speed of 50 mph. He admitted heavy rain in the preceding month may have affected the ground generally, but not, it was stated, in the vicinity of Gomshall.

Taking into account the evidence of the passing times of the train at the previous signal boxes and even allowing for the inaccuracies that can occur from these, the inspecting officer was forced to concede that the 50 mph speed was in fact the most likely, with the track simply not in a suitable condition for such working. Blame was attributed solely against the driver although it was noted that the SECR should if necessary set the timing of trains so their services could run with due allowance made for any necessary restrictions placed due to the condition of the track. (The previous train to use the line had been a stopping service earlier that day which passed over the crossing at 10 mph without incident.)

Including the driver and fireman of No. 284, six persons were injured, four seriously. Damage being caused to the engine and tender plus the first three vehicles of the train. In view of the fact that the body of at least one passenger coach was torn from its chassis it is indeed fortunate there were no fatalities. Locomotive No. 284 was repaired and lasted until 1911.

'O' No. 284

HALWILL JUNCTION - 16 June 1944

'N' No. 1833

The accident at Halwill Junction on 16 June 1944 was both unfortunate and spectacular. Unfortunate because it came about through what might almost be described as a comical set of circumstances and spectacular due to the amount of effort required to recover the locomotive involved.

As with so many incidents the facts are simply told. No 1833 left the up platform at Halwill Junction accelerating hard with its train - we are not told what service was involved but it may be assumed to have been a heavy freight. The crew were attempting to gain as much speed as possible for the climb to Ashbury (an initial descent at 1-330 which steepened to 1 in 75 down for a short distance before commencing a severe climb for some miles at 1 in 132/78/80). A new loop, officially the up siding, had recently been laid in leaving Halwill this to cope with increased traffic, the train being routed this way.

Whether taking this loop line caused any confusion on the footplate is not reported but there was certainly some concern when the crew realised that at the end of the loop instead of being turned back out on to the single line the points were instead set for the dead end. Despite a valiant attempt by the driver to check his speed the train continued past the points up a short spur before nose-diving down on to the Beaworthy Road which crossed under the main line at this point. It was indeed fortunate that the road was clear. Recovery was difficult to say the least, as is described in the accompanying illustrations.

Opposite top - *No. 1833 lies straddling the Beaworthy Road. Above the locomotive the ground frame controlling the exit points may be seen.*

Opposite bottom - *The tender from No. 1833 was able to be recovered partly by crane, but recovery of the locomotive would prove to be somewhat more difficult. Clearly a warm day from the jackets hanging across what was bridge No. 19 sign.*

Above - *Having been partly recovered by the crane, the tender is hauled back to a more usual angle. The short distance between the crossover that should have been taken, and the end of the spur will be noted.*

It was quickly established that cranes could not be used to recover the engine and instead it would be a question of hauling it back to the level of the spur from whence it could be righted. Having dug out the ground as much possible to form a slope, two engines, a USA 'S160' and an 'S15', were specially permitted to cross Meldon Viaduct for the attempt. A ships hawser was used for strength but even on a second attempt and with the assistance of a third engine, another member of the 'N' class, the only result was damage to the 'S160'.

A revised plan was evolved using a greased plate being placed under* No. 1833 whilst five engines, 2 x 4-6-0 and 3 x 2-6-0 managed to recover the engine. It was repaired and saw service for several more years.

The images are from the collection of Jeremy Cobb) and had an interesting note attached. "To Locomotive Running Supt. Deepdene (Mr Cobb Snr. Held the latter position). Herewith photographs taken by Mr Steel and his representatives."

Whilst bearing an official 'Southern Railway Copyright Free' stamp on the reverse their quality is perhaps not quite up to the normal official type, indicate that during wartime at formal record images of this type may have been taken by any member of staff who happened to be present.

All Jeremy Cobb collection.

* we may rightly wonder how this was placed.

BRIGHTON, 29th JANUARY

At 11.23 a.m. *when* the 8.50 a.m. steam train from Victoria to Brighton, via Eridge and Lewes, which consisted of three coaches, entered No. 9 platform road at Brighton, it collided slightly with five empty coaches which were standing adjacent to the buffer stops. Three of the stationary vehicles were slightly damaged.

No complaints of shook or injury were received from passengers, but Guard Botting, who was riding in the rear coach, sustained a blow on the head, which did not, however, prevent him from continuing duty.

Driver Russell stated that the Brighton up East Branch home signal was shewing a one yellow aspect, together with route indicator No.9, and he therefore expected to find the platform road partially occupied. He entered the platform at about four to five miles per hour, but his view was obstructed by a curve and an engine attached to a train in No. 8 road. On observing the stock standing on No.9 road, Russell applied the brake but was unable to avoid a slight impact.

A joint enquiry was held and the Officers reported as follows:-"We find that Driver Russell is responsible for the collision in that after having passed the home signal showing the yellow aspect, he failed to stop clear of the stock in the platform."

"There is no evidence to show that the Driver entered the platform at an excessive speed, and in view of the difficulty of observation due to the curve and to the stock and engine standing in the adjacent road, we can only attribute the mishap to a slight error of judgment on Russell's part." Driver Russell has been reprimanded.

It transpires that the train could have been run to No.10 platform, which was unoccupied, and Signalman Cole has been given some suitable advice in this connection.

ELMERS END 31st JANUARY

At 7.19 a.m when the 7.10 a.m. electric train from Hayes to Elmers End, which consisted of three coaches, entered the down bay platform at the latter station, it came in contact with the buffer stops which were displaced, the guard irons on the leading motor coach of the train also being damaged. No complaints were received from passengers. The mishap was due to an error of judgment on the part of Motorman Cooper, who has been suitably dealt with.

WATERLOO 31st JANUARY

At 9.34 a.m. the 8.48 a.m. electric train from Windsor, which consisted of six coaches, came in contact with the hydraulic buffer stops of No. 21 platform road at Waterloo, the stops being driven in to the extent of about four feet.

No damage was caused to the train and no complaints were received from passengers.

The Guard states that the train appeared to be well under control when entering Waterloo and the mishap was due to an error of judgment on the part of Driver (Acting Motorman) Williams, who has been reprimanded.

SLADES GREEN, 12th JANUARY.

The 4. 6 p.m. electric train from Slades Green to Cannon Street, which consisted of eight coaches, ran throughout the journey with the Westinghouse automatic brake inoperative on the last two coaches, owing to the cock in the train pipe being closed at the leading end of the seventh coach.

The train had arrived at Slades Green Sheds after the morning services on the 12th January, and some attention was given to the brakes, which work was carried out between 11.30 and 11.45 a.m. On completion of the work Foreman Fitter Davidson states the brake was tested throughout the train and found to be in order.

At 2.35 p.m. Shed Motorman Snell moved the train from the shed, driving from the leading motor cab at the London end, and noticed nothing amiss.

At 3.40 p.m. Guard Loman, who was to work the 4. 6 p.m. service from Slades Green, discovered that the train pipe cock at the rear end of the trailer set was closed, thus isolating the rear unit. Loman opened this and shortly afterwards informed Motorman Williams. Although both men had their suspicions aroused and looked round the train they failed to see that the second cock was closed. When testing the brake Guard Loman did so from an intermediate van instead of the rear van.

Loman was riding in the rear Guard's compartment of the leading unit in consequence of the up platforms at Erith and Belvedere not being of sufficient length to accommodate the whole of the eight car train, and instructions are in force that, in order to avoid pulling up the train, passengers for those stations must be loaded in the front part of the train and that the Guard must ride in the rear brake van of the front unit throughout the journey.

During the journey to Cannon Street Motorman Williams states that although the brake required a little more air than usual, no difficulty was experienced. At Cannon Street the Motorman and Guard changed ends, Loman being relieved by Guard Farthing, and as the gauge in what was then the rear van only showed 45 lbs. Farthing made a test, which sent the needle to zero, at which point it remained. An examination of the train was then made and the train pipe cock at the buffer stop end of the middle coach of the front unit was found to be shut.

A joint enquiry was held and the Officers reported as follows:- "Despite searching investigation, we have been unable to establish by whom the two cocks were turned. Being turned either side of one coach, it

Continued on page 77

HITHER GREEN - 20 February 1960

'Battle of Britain' No. 34084

In the early morning of 20 February 1960, No. 34084 *'253 Squadron'* ran out of rails after failing to stop at the end of the up goods loop at Hither Green. The engine had been in charge of a Dover Marine to Bricklayer's Arms van train.

A short run-off siding at the end of the loop had been provided to prevent a run-past such as this from fouling the main line, although the margin for safety was short and certainly insufficient to prevent No. 34084 from continuing on as it ran out of track and fell to one side.

It was indeed fortunate that the speed involved was low, although even so the coal office nearby had a narrow escape.

Fortunately none of the running lines were blocked but there was considerable disruption to services, a number of signalling cables having been severed. Temporary signalling repairs were made as a matter of priority with service able to pass as normal the following day.

In many respects this incident was similar to that experienced at Shawford in 1952 - see page 78 - consequently the expertise of Stephen Townroe from Eastleigh was called upon. He advised a similar approach to that successfully taken at Shawford indeed his method of dealing with such incidents had been, and would be, used elsewhere on BR. What this involved was clearing away a path underneath the recalcitrant machine whilst naturally preventing further movement. The vital part was that the wheels and tyres were exposed, at which stage lengths of bull-head rail were tied on to the edge of the tyres but with the rail turned through 90° compared with how it would be laid for normal running - see image top-left on page 55. The wheel tyres of the engine were thus in a grove. When the engine was restored to a vertical position the wheels would then initially run in these metal grooves.

When the engine was then restored to the vertical

again, the lengths of bull-head rail referred to were attached, suitably packed, to normal rail sections temporarily laid backwards to the end of the siding. The engine was then firmly held to prevent it rolling forward after which the attachment made by the ties holding the turned bull-head rail to the wheels would be removed. The engine could then be pulled, or as was more normal, winched with Kelbus or similar gear back to safety. ('Kelbus' was an arrangement of wires and pulleys allowing for the haulage of very heavy loads through a system of low gear pulleys.)

Removal of the train behind No. 34084 was easily accomplished although the urgent task was to stabilise the engine and prevent any further movement. This was initially achieved with timber packing, invariably sleepers, placed under the solid side of the Bulleid smokebox. Following this the boiler casing was removed and ties attached to the boiler. Hydraulic jacks were then placed against suitable points on these ties, the jacks themselves supported on sleepers against the ground.

The casing of a Bulleid pacific was of course insufficient to take much weight on its own and it was simply removed, possibly by the straightforward expedience of cutting it away. In so doing much asbestos insulation was exposed - but this was before the days the dangers of such material were fully appreciated. An extra difficulty was the oil which had escaped from the oil-bath of No. 34084: this then ignited - there were no doubt several ready sources of ignition in the immediate aftermath. (Did the local coal merchant benefit from the spill of coal from the tender....!)

Digging out could now begin, much of this having to be done by hand. Even so it was completed in just a few days and rails were attached to the wheels, as described earlier. A solid foundation of sleepers was also added on to which No. 34084 would eventually be rolled over.

It had been intended to recover the engine on 24

February but fate lent a hand with the derailment of diesel-shunter nearby. The breakdown crew therefore had to attend to this instead, although the drawbar between the engine and tender of No. 34084 and the tender itself was removed the same day.

A second, this time successful, attempt was made on Sunday 28 February, eight days after the incident. Two cranes, those from Stewarts Lane and Bricklayers Arms were used. These, together the aid of the jacks referred to, pulled the engine to the vertical and by 3.30 pm it was restored to the rails.

No. 34084 was examined, the damage more superficial than serious. It was towed to Eastleigh and repaired there in April of the same year.

Eleven years earlier the same engine had been one of a pair of 'Battle of Britain' engines involved in a 'coming together' outside Victoria - see Issue No 3 of 'The Southern Way'.

Concluding the story of No. 34084, the engine hauled the last steam hauled weekday up 'Atlantic Coast Express' between Bude and Exeter on Friday 14 August 1964. It was withdrawn from Eastleigh shed on 3 October 1965, but stored there until February 1966 when it towed to South Wales being scrapped by Buttigiegs at Newport in March 1966. No. 34084 had a life of slightly less than 18 years. The final mileage run was 663,249.

With thanks to the relatives of Mr Brooker (ex Stewarts Lane Breakdown Gang) and Patrick Collett. Colour images only R E Vincent / The Transport Treasury. See also 'Steam World' March 2004 - article by Nigel Harris.

This page, top left - The rails tied to the driving and bogie wheels may be noted as is the solid sleeper foundation on to which No. 34084 will be pulled / rolled. **Bottom -** *No 34084 awaiting repair Eastleigh on 9 March 1960. Peter Cleare / KR collection.*

'M7' No. 30480

Both views: S C Townroe / R Blencowe collection

Reproduced from the 'Meccano Magazine' for May 1954 under the title: 'A Job for the Breakdown Crane' by S C Townroe.

"Early one Sunday morning, when our household was enjoying that extra hour in bed, the telephone awakened me. "This is Control," said the speaker, and went on to say that an (Up) passenger train on the rural single line from Winchester Junction to Alton had broken down in the section between Itchen Abbas and Alresford.

"The driver had walked to Alresford Station, where he telephoned to tell Control that his engine. No. 30480, an 0-4-4 tank, was immobilised with a broken tyre on the right driving wheel. He had succeeded in stopping the train without further mishap, at a point some 1½ miles west of Alresford.

"Control's first thought was for the passengers. Fortunately, the Hants and Dorset Company had been able to provide a bus almost at once from their Winchester garage, and this was already on its way to pick up the stranded passengers.

"Now when an engine comes to grief with a mechanical defect on a single line it is always a difficult proposition to deal with, especially when, as in this instance, a crane is needed to lift the engine in order to effect repairs. The train was a pull-and-push one and the engine was pushing at the time, so the breakdown crane would have to approach it in the up direction.

"This was not a case where the breakdown train could proceed at full speed to the scene. Arrangements would have to be made for its engine to run round it before entering the single line, and then to propel the crane head-on for six miles* until it reached the crippled engine. Such a movement would, moreover, have to be made under special authority, to permit entry into the section already occupied by the stationary train.

"Meanwhile the foreman of the gang went ahead with me, by car, to examine luckless No. 30480. We saw that the broken tyre was very loose and would have to be removed on the spot. In the rare event of a breakage, the tension in the tyre causes it to spring open slightly. Obviously No. 30480 had run some distance with the brakes hard on before stopping, and the tyre had opened considerably in the process. And with some bumping!

"A series of exploding detonators, placed in accordance with the Rules to protect a disabled train, heralded the arrival of the crane. The front of No. 30480 was lifted sufficiently to take the coupled wheels off the rails, after the coupling rods had been removed, while an oxy-acetylene torch was used to cut the tyre into three pieces. On rotating the driving axle with crowbars, the pieces of tyre then fell to the side of the track.

"The next operation was to place packing on top of the axle-boxes of the leading wheels; by this means, when the engine had been lowered by the crane, the driving wheels remained clear of the rails by an inch or so. The engine was then movable on six of its eight wheels, although not exactly 'on an even keel'! Finally, as it was slowly towed away by the breakdown train, the small crowd of spectators watched it disappear, and then went home, like us, to Sunday dinner."

* This means the crane would have been pulled to Winchester, the engine run-round and the crane propelled from there on. (Some years later, long after M7s and push-pull working had been replaced by DEMU trains on the Alton line, the motor coach of a DEMU set was derailed when it hit a cow at almost the exact same point.)

'D' No. 360

The runaway accident at the terminus at Littlehampton which occurred at 1.32 pm on Wednesday 4 August 1920, was a simple matter of a train running away due to the brakes not having been correctly connected. Several railway employees were culpable, all of these being identified by the Board of Trade inspecting officer although their subsequent fate, so far as their position or even their employment by the LBSCR is not reported. From the illustrations seen (one of which has in the past been incorrectly attributed to an engine falling into a turntable pit), the occupants of the houses had a lucky escape. We are not told if they had been indoors to witness the engine bearing down upon them.

The train involved was the 1.10 pm from the station at Ford Junction to Littlehampton, consisting of the engine seen, running bunker first, immediately followed by two 8-wheel trailer cars (it is relevant that these were motor fitted but were not in use as a motor train), a 6-wheel brake-van, and then five other 6-wheel vehicles. The Westinghouse brake was fitted to all the vehicles of the train. There were about 30 passengers on board: 13 suffered minor injuries or shock. The driver and fireman managed to jump clear just before the impact.

At Ford Junction (in later years known simply as 'Ford') the train had arrived from Arundel, meaning the engine had to be uncoupled and then run-round for the final leg of the journey to Littlehampton. Driver Edwards

stated he had no difficulty in stopping but did notice he had used more air, approx 30lbs, than might have been usual. Meanwhile the engine was uncoupled from the train by Porter Dinnage: normally it would have been a shunter who performed this task but at meal times the work was devolved to the porter on duty, Dinnage confirmed he had 'continuous experience' but had never received any instructions from either the shunters or station foreman. The engine ran-round and at the same time Porter Dinnage walked to the opposite end of the platform ready to re-attach it to the train.

There was some difficulty in getting the engine screw coupling to reach on to the coach and so to ensure no further movement, he first opened the tap on the train-pipe of car No 1327 - now the leading coach - and called on the driver to set back. With the engine to coach coupling made and quoting from the official report, "...he reached over the coupling and took hold of the engine hose pipe with his right hand; he then took hold of the second hose pipe coupling, counting from the side of the car furthest from the platform, with his left hand, connected them over the screw coupling and opened their respective taps. He heard the sound of air passing through the pipes, but could not say whether release of the brake blocks on the coaches was effected. Nor did he remember whether there was the usual clicking noise of the brakes releasing....... He mentioned it was difficult to read the

name plates of the hose pipes, especially on trailer cars fitted, as in this case, with a vestibule." Ignorance now came into play as Dinnage admitted he did not know it would make any difference which of the two centre hose pipes on the car was connected to the engine pipe and that the only reason for selecting that particular coupling was that he had noticed hose couplings always cross the screw coupling when they are connected!

The train remained at Ford owing to a late arrival from Brighton and instead of leaving at the scheduled 1.10 pm it was delayed until 1.27pm.

Guard Fribbins is the next player, he confirmed he watched the train gauge rise more slowly than usual, from 20lbs to 70lbs. He was not concerned about the slow rise in pressure as earlier that day there had been an air leak from a control lever in the other trailer car, No. 1336. Despite the appropriate valve being tightened by the driver, this leak was considered by the driver to be the cause as to why it had been necessary to use more air on stopping at Ford and also why it had been necessary to maintain the locomotive brake-handle in the 'full-charge' rather than the 'running' position, the former meaning the Westinghouse pump would have been operating continuously.

The run to Littlehampton was made at a maximum speed of about 25mph. Driver Edwards first applied the brake in the vicinity of the outer home signal, but to no effect. He applied the brake more fully again but again to no effect at which point the fireman screwed the handbrake on. Applying the train brake fully and again to no effect Edwards realised the error and called out "We are on the wrong pipe", the fireman now applying the hand brake as hard as possible. Edwards now reversed the

engine and applied steam, all of which managed to reduce speed from about 25 mph when passing the station signal box to about 15 mph half way along the platform and to 8 mph when the engine struck the buffers. He admitted he did not whistle for the guard to assist with his hand-brake nor had he tested the brake when passing the distant signal.

Driver Edwards admitted that at Ford a few weeks earlier, he had found it necessary to advise the porter (we learn later this was in fact a passenger shunter) when an incorrect air connection had been made. On this occasions the Ford station master was advised of the error but he in turn only told the other passenger shunter and not the porters. In the absence of the station master, as had occurred on 4 August, the station foreman at Ford should have ensured the correct connections had been made. These three men, driver, guard, and station foreman were the ones who were considered by the inspector at fault, Porter Dinnage's actions seen as ones of ignorance by a man with only 10 months service and who had received no proper training.

The recommendations were clear, ensure compliance with the rules; Removal of hoses not in use*; and / or different size couplings so that incorrect connections could not be made.
* According to Mr Horne the Ford Junction station master, motor stock had not been used on the LBSCR since 1916 and had only been re-introduced about June 1920 and then only to strengthen ordinary trains. (This could go some way to explaining the unfamiliarity by the shunters, although no mention was made by the Inspector that a simply remedy would have been for the LBSCR to remove all the redundant hoses.)

LONDON BRIDGE - 11 November 1953

'4SUB No. 4102' plus unknown EMU

The incident outside London Bridge on the morning of 11 November 1953 is curious because, to date, no report or reference to the occurrence has been located in official paperwork. Indeed had it not been for the illustration above and associated notes on the rear, it would have remained an accident almost forgotten and so unrecorded.

What little it has been possible to glean therefore comes from the rear of the photographs and reports as follows, "Ambulances and rescue teams of firemen were called to London Bridge station today, after two trains had collided. One of the trains, coming from Tattenham Corner, was approaching the station, when another Southern Region train crashed into it. The Tattenham Corner train was derailed, but fortunately there were no casualties, although some of the passengers were treated for shock. The photograph shows the scene of the crash this morning."

On the extreme left notice the person's head peering out of the window - a stranded passenger perhaps? Further information on this incident would be appreciated.

MAZE HILL

MAZE HILL - 4 July 1958

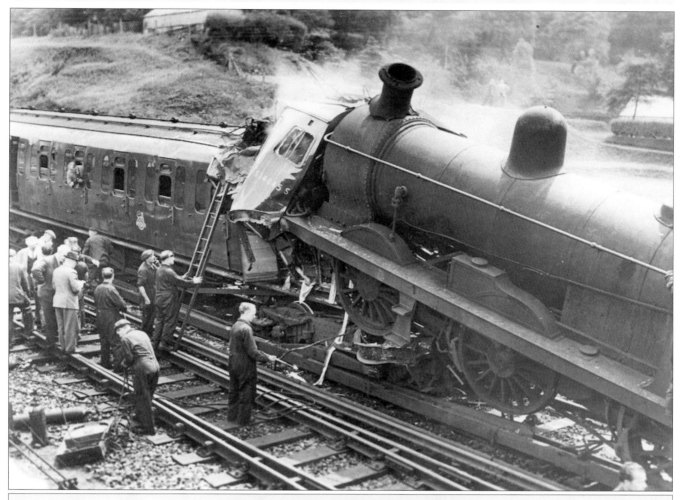

'C' No. 31461 and '4-EPB' set No. 5023

On the morning of 4 July 1958, the 9.41 am 10-car Gravesend - Charing Cross electric service collided head-on with 'C' No. 31461 which was itself at the head of a nine-coach empty passenger train. The steam train was in the process of legitimately shunting from the up sidings across the up line towards the down line when it was struck by the electric train, whose driver despite admitting he passed the up distant signal at 'on', failed to observe the Maze Hill up home signal at danger. Having seen the steam engine ahead, the driver of the EMU succeeded in reducing his speed from 40 to 25 mph at the point of collision, although this still created enough force at the actual impact sufficient to push the empty train backwards for 11 yards and lift the front of the steam engine which in turn mounted the leading coach of the electric train.

The up and down lines were immediately blocked and the electric current cut off automatically by a heavy short circuit. There were about 50 passengers in the electric train, 43 of these, together with the guard, were taken to hospital. From the damage seen, Motorman P W Hurst was fortunate to have escaped death, although he too was taken to hospital. Five persons were detained, but none was seriously injured.

EPB motor coach S14045S from No. 5023 was still present at Maze Hill on 13 July, although the remainder of the set had been moved to Slade Green on 10 July. Set No. 5023 was not reformed, its remaining vehicles initially used as spares. Inspection of No. 31461 revealed it was not considered worthy of repair and consequently was officially withdrawn in August 1958 although it unlikely it ever worked again following the accident. The driver of the electric service was charged with endangering public safety and tried at the Old Bailey. He was though found not guilty and acquitted.

Illustrations courtesy Andy Gibbs / Pete Beyer

MAZE HILL - 4 July 1958

MIDHURST - COCKING - 9 September 1904

'D' No. 239

The derailment, for that is exactly what is was, that occurred sometime after 3.00 pm on Friday 9 September 1904 has been reported on previously elsewhere. Recounting the incident might thus appear strange except that is for additional information that has become available, which together with the full collection of views available from the archives of the late R C Riley, present a far more complete selection than has previously been published. Accordingly there is little excuse needed for the inclusion of this derailment.

On the afternoon of the day in question, the 3.00 pm goods left Midhurst as usual for Singleton. According to Paul Clark in his excellent 'The Chichester and Midhurst Railway' book, the train consisted of an open truck, box van and guard's van although it is not completely clear if this was the formation for the trip out from Midhurst, for both the out and back workings, or for just the return trip. In any event it is with the return working with which we are concerned.

The due arrival time for the goods to return to Midhurst came and went and thus to try and ascertain what might have occurred - communication with the signal box down the line would have confirmed the train had left and should indeed be on the way back so a breakdown may well have been suspected - 'a messenger' was despatched from Midhurst to walk along the track and so hopefully meet or locate the missing service. (The Rule Book states that if a train is an unusually long time 'in-section' the signalman should take steps to attempt to ascertain the cause. In practise this would mean advising the station master who in turn would instruct probably the junior porter to investigate. As the whereabouts of the train were completely unknown at this stage it could well have been that a 'search party' was similarly being sent from Singleton.)

It was the man from Midhurst who located the train, the engine, No. 239 'Patcham' lying at an angle in soft ground just north of the Park Lane bridge, opposite

the turning for Heyshott. The three wagons of the train had also been thrown off the rails and all were damaged to varying degree.

According to the driver, the engine "...had been coasting towards Midhurst about 20 mph when it inexplicably left the rails." He continued, that steam had been immediately shut off and the engine reversed but the train travelled another 100 yards, tearing the track as it went, before coming to rest. The open wagon immediately behind overturned across the line, the box van went down on the opposite side of the embankment and the guard's van was "quite badly smashed up and spun round back to front". Both the driver and firemen remained at their place on the footplate during the incident, the guard reported as flinging himself to the floor and being lucky to escape with just cuts, bruises and an obvious shaking. We are not told if the loco crew were physically injured. But even from the above one question applies, was it an automatic reaction by the driver to reverse the engine after it had left the rails? If the account above is a true representation then once the wheels were 'tearing up the rails' neither reversing the engine nor braking would have had the slightest effect.

It was reported that men worked through the night to repair the track so that services might resume the next day.

Unfortunately despite the above additional detail on the initial cause, no formal explanation as to the cause is given and with the passage of years it is unlikely this will now ever be known. The obvious options are speed, track, mechanical failure, or obstruction and whilst there is an amount of detail that may be gleaned from the images, the fact the track had been repaired by the time the views were taken means any clue that might be gained from a visual appearance is gone.

Recovery was scheduled to take place two days later on 11 September, news of the occasion meaning a sizeable crowd gathered to watch the proceedings - it was not every day there was such free entertainment! The railway company also took the view that maintaining a service to passengers was most important, even on what was already a minor branch line, consequently any passengers were to be inconvenienced as little as possible.

So, on the day the line was blocked for the recovery, the 3.30 pm Midhurst to Chichester was deliberately run in two halves. One half took passengers from Midhurst as far as the location where the cranes were working, the public then alighting and walking past the

site of work to the other side where a second train was waiting to allow them to continue their journey.

Two steam cranes were brought in, one from Brighton and the other from New Cross, recovery of the damaged wagons accomplished without undue difficulty.

Recovering the engine though took no less than three attempts, the first failed due to the chain attached to the front of the engine snapping, whilst the next saw the Brighton crane starting to tip as it took the weight - a prompt order to lower saved the crane as well as an embarrassing and potentially dangerous situation.

'Patcham' was later successfully re-railed and towed to Brighton for repair.

NEW CROSS - 6 January 1923

Metropolitan Electric Train and LNER 0-6-0T

New Cross, January 1923 is included as being at a Southern Railway location (just one week earlier it would been an LBSCR station) even if the locomotive and stock involved were not of SR origin. The incident occurred in the station itself and whilst no images have been found of the damaged LNER locomotive and 6-wheel brake-van, there were in an old photograph album the attached views, including that above conveniently annotated as to the 'point of collision'. The inclusion of the others does not call for much excuse either, wonderful contemporary views of the electric train involved and of course the general railway scene.

About 6.18 am on the day in question, the 6.06 am Metropolitan electric from Shoreditch was running into the East London line platform at New Cross. In so doing it collided, fortunately at low speed, with an LNER engine and van standing at the starting signal of the same platform but waiting to leave (bunker-first) in the opposite direction to that of the in-coming train. Damage to the steam engine, details of which are not given, was confined to the buffer beam and left hand side of the footplate. The electric train suffered broken headstocks, damaged equipment generally, damaged ends and buckled solebars. At that time the passenger count was fortunately low, just five or six persons. But in proportionate terms the injury list was high: three passengers, the motorman

and guard of the electric service and one of the guards in the brake van attached to the steam engine.

The cause of the accident was a signalling error in that following the departure of an earlier East London line service from the relevant platform, the engine and van were legitimately put into the same platform by the South signal box. Signalman Pattenden at this box was then offered the electric train, having now but forgotten about the LNER engine the stage was set.

The driver of the electric train, William Wedge, saw the lights of the standing engine in front of him as he approached the platform, but admits he did not realise it was on the same line as him, thinking quite naturally it must be on an adjacent siding. Realising the danger he made an emergency application of the brake, whilst simultaneously the driver of the waiting steam engine, William Mead, saw the situation developing and jumped on to the platform displaying a red light to the approaching train. The collision followed almost immediately.

Matters night have been saved had the signalmen involved been more alert to the workings, notwithstanding the fact that both had booking-boys, one of whom later admitted than the 'obstruction removed' and subsequent 'train accepted' entries were put in by guess work. When investigated it was found that such a short train was not long enough to ensure that any part of it was standing on the fouling bar along the platform line, consequently it was all too easy to forget the presence of the train.

Major Hall, the Inspecting Officer, made the obvious comment that track-circuiting should be applied to the platform line, noting also that the existing signalling, electrical circuitry and type of working at New Cross had been altered so much in the 30 years since it was installed that, "...neither the type of instrument nor the circuits are such as would have been installed by the manufacturers originally, or supplied at the present time, for the purpose for which they are used." A polite way of saying they were no longer fit for purpose. New Cross was in effect a wake-up call, it was just fortunate it was not more serious than it had been

RYDE - 2 June 1965

'O2' No. W22

Notwithstanding the obvious run-down of steam and with it the railway network on the Isle of Wight by the mid-1960s, there was still a considerable passenger service south from Ryde in the summer of 1965. Most of this was on the route to Ventnor but add to it the traffic still using the Cowes route and the need to run to as close to time as possible due to restrictions on line occupancy beyond Smallbrook Junction and it becomes apparent that even the slightest disruption could throw the whole operation into turmoil.

One of these unfortunate events took place on Wednesday 2 June 1965 when No. 22 'Brading' managed to 'fall off' whilst using the crossover on Ryde Pier immediately south of the station. One can almost imagine the consternation felt by the crew, signalman, duty inspector and of course passengers. Visually it would appear to be a relatively simple matter for the nearby Ryde works breakdown crew to deal with, but without further information we cannot of course speculate on the cause. (Sometimes such events were caused by the simple matter of all wishing to get the job done as fast as possible and cutting the odd corner but with the best intentions.)

Whatever, No. 22 would certainly have been inspected to ascertain the derailment had not been caused by a more sinister occurance, mechanical defect, axlebox, bearing etc, fortunately it would appear not, for it was certainly back and running again shortly afterwards being one of the final batch of O2's to be withdrawn (excepting of course the two temporarily retained for engineering purposes) at the end of December 1966.

Mike Morant

ST DENYS - 29 October 1959

'West Country' No. 34020

How are the mighty fallen. On 29 October 1959 Bulleid's proud light Pacific No 34020 *Seaton* was travelling on the up local line approaching St Denys with the 6.30 pm. Weymouth to Waterloo train when the driver misread the signals. Those for the up through line were clear, his was not. Consequently No. 34020 ran through the trap points ending up in soft ground at the end of the up platform ramp. When photographed the train and tender had been removed, although the engine was still

there two days later. With speed restrictions in force traffic was able to continue.

Recovery was made slightly more onerous as soft ground at the end of the sand-drag meant that every time the back of the loco was lifted the front sank further. Two cranes were eventually used although as this was a heavily trafficked main line, recovery could not take place until a full possession could be obtained. (At least three similar incidents occurred here involving drivers misreading the up through line signal as applicable to the local line. Two were in the 1930s, one involving a lucky escape. On that occasion a Portsmouth-bound train was routed via the local line to wait until a boat train had passed on the up main. The driver of the Portsmouth train on misreading the signal not only continued into the sand-drag but by a fluke dislocated the point rodding meaning the up boat train was diverted on to the Portsmouth route. This was indeed fortunate as the derailed engine had fouled the main line. It was lucky too there was nothing travelling in the opposite, down, direction. Then on 12 December 1960, No. 34022 replicated exactly the story of No. 34020 - excepting that the up main line was also foul. On this occasion recovery was undertaken immediately.   Colin Boocock

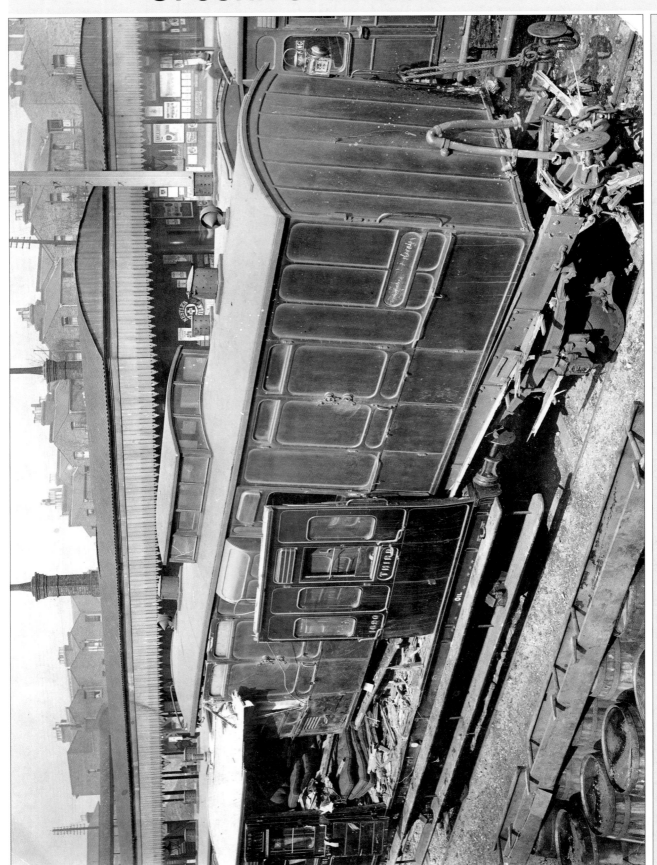

'THIRD CLASS' CARRIAGE No. 1690 and 'BRAKE VAN' No. 289

About 9.00 am on a foggy Monday 21 March 1897, the 7.45 am train from Tonbridge to London was standing at the up home signal at St John's when it was run into by the 7.00 am service from Hastings. Regrettably three persons were killed and although officially only 20 persons were reported as injured, many others complained of being 'shaken' - a contemporary euphemism for shock.

The accident was investigated for the Board of Trade by Lieut. Col. G W Addison, who quickly established the fault lay in the part of signalman Honey at St John's who, having legitimately accepted the Tonbridge train into his section, had it standing at his signals and then forgot it. Whether this was compounded by poor visibility that morning, and / or busy working on other lines is not reported.

`Whatever, he was then offered the Hastings service and being unable to release his signals due to the Sykes lock-and-block system, made the fatal error of using his release key. There appears to have been some justification for this as the treadle provided had reportedly failed on a number of previous occasions and resource to the release key was thus a fairly common occurrence.

Unfortunately on this this occasion the system was locked for legitimate reasons - the Tonbridge train - and by using his release the scene was thus set. Other contributory factors may have played a part, not least of which was the presence of a booking boy in the signal box but he did not feel he could overrule the signalman. After this the result was sadly inevitable.

In the view opposite, clearly taken after the accident, the damaged stock of the Tonbridge train has been brought forward into the sidings adjacent to the up main platform, the two last vehicles of the Tonbridge train being placed in the most westerly siding.

The accident report confirms the make up of the Tonbridge train to have been eight coaches with a van at each end, whilst the Hastings service consisted of six passenger coaches and two vans at the rear. Although the engine number and type hauling the Hastings service are not given, enough information is provided to confirm this as a 4-4-0 We are also told damage to this service was minimal so much so that none of the vehicles left the rails.

Notwithstanding his culpability, Lieut. Col. Addison was at pains to point out Honey's admission as to his fault.

EXTRACTS FROM THE SR TRAFFIC COMMITTEE 1933
continued from page 51

continued from page 51

would at first sight seem that it was done by design, but had it been necessary to isolate one coach for any purpose we should certainly have expected the cooks to be turned on the coach itself and not on the coaches either side of it."

"We accept Foreman Fitter Davidson's statement that the brake was tested when the work on the brake blocks was completed and therefore conclude that the turning of the cocks must have been done subsequent to 11.45 a.m."

"It may actually have been the case that the brakes were in order when the train was prepared for service by Motorman Snell and it is difficult to say therefore whether any blame rests with him. In the circumstances he must be given the benefit of the doubt."

"It is, of course, because of the possibility of happenings like this that the brake test is necessary, and the primary responsibility therefore rests with Guard Loman in that by applying the brake from an intermediate van he only made a partial test.

"Motorman Williams is also at fault for not having detected the closed cock when looking round the train."

Guard Loman and Motorman Williams have been reprimanded.

WHITE HART LEVEL CROSSING, BETWEEN BARNES AND MORTLAKE, l5th JANUARY.

At 8.32 p.m. a motor car collided with the left hand gate on the up side of the line at White Hart Level Crossing as the 8,15 p.m. train from Hounslow to Waterloo, via Twickenham, which consisted of six coaches, was passing the Crossing. The gate was struck by the second coach and smashed, damage also being caused to the second, third and fourth coaches of the train.

The Signalman at White Hart Crossing at once forwarded the "stop and examine train" signal to Barnes Junction, and on arrival at Barnes the train was examined. After a delay of three minutes it was allowed to proceed cautiously to Waterloo, where the front unit was taken out of service.

The crossing gates had been closed across the roadway two minutes prior to the mishap. Two red lamps, one on each pair of gates, are provided. The lamps were alight and in good order and with the gates across the roadway would be visible to Drivers of vehicles approaching the crossing on the up line side at a distance of about 100 yards. The lamp on the right hand gate on the up side was still burning after the mishap.

The car, which was being driven by Mr. A.D. Antiquis, contained three other persons, but no one was injured.

It is understood that the Metropolitan Police are taking proceedings against the Driver of the car, and arrangements are being made to render an account to him in respect of the costs incurred by the Company.

SHAWFORD - 20 July 1952

SOUTHERN REGION
DERAILMENT AT SHAWFORD (HANTS)
20th. JULY, 1952
(Relevant signals only, shown)

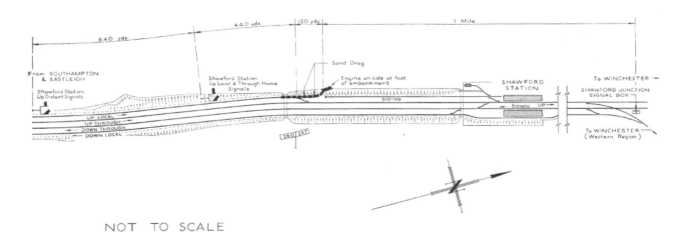

NOT TO SCALE

'Lord Nelson' No. 30854

The accident at Shawford on Sunday 20 July 1952 has been recounted in the past using colour material taken by Stephen Townroe. Here though for what is believed to be the first time, is his b/w imagery of the event together with his own description of the incident as appeared in the '*Meccano Magazine*' for March 1953.

Before recounting the latter a brief summary of the occurrence from the official Ministry of Transport report may be appropriate. The story itself is briefly told. On the day in question, the 3.24 pm Southampton Central to Waterloo passenger train - seven coaches hauled by No. 30854 '*Howard of Effingham*' left Eastleigh routed via the up local line: this was in order to give precedence to a Southampton to Waterloo boat train.

No. 30854 passed the up (Otterbourne) local distant signal at danger and then continued past the

associated home signal, also at danger, before running on for a further 560 yards to enter the sand-drag at the end of the up local line beyond which it overturned down a 20' embankment. Fortunately the coaching stock remained upright and there were no casualties - not even from the engine crew.

No defects were found affecting the engine, track or signaling and this was a clear case of human error. The driver was totally honest in this, commenting that after passing the distant signal at caution he slowed gently and on rounding the curve leading to the bracket on which were placed the two home signals (up local and up through) saw the latter (that for the main line) in the 'off' position. He admitted later that what he had actually seen was just one signal arm displayed, the other obstructed by smoke from the engine - poor coal was reported as being fired - and consequently seeing this signal at 'off' assumed it was for him. He also admitted that he had never been routed on the local line before.

Little else in the report need be mentioned, although both the guard and assistant guard were criticized for perhaps not taking action themselves. Both stated they saw their respective vacuum gauges drop as the brakes were initially applied and would then naturally have had little concern the driver was not in control. Their behaviour in not taking action had they noticed they had passed the stop signal at danger may be more open to criticism. There were still over 500 yards to try and recover the matter, whether this would have enough is debatable.

Regardless of earlier inaction, the head guard of the derailed train did manage to regain some credit by laying down detonators and with a red flag managed to stop the approaching boat train travelling at 50 - 55 mph (hauled by No. 30749 'Iseult' with 250 passengers on board). Passengers from the derailed train were transferred to this service at Shawford station a short distance further on.

Opposite and above - *The tender of No 30854 lies at an angle down the embankment at the end of the sand. Fortunately there was no obstruction to the main running lines, thus with the upright coaches from the derailed train drawn clear and taken back to Eastleigh, the up local line was able to be restored to traffic at 6.24 pm, less than two hours after the derailment. Bill Bishops's records indicate that the Eastleigh breakdown crane was ready to leave the depot at 6.00pm but such was the volume of traffic that it took until 6.52pm before they reached the site - just four miles away. They again had to wait but eventually succeeded in re-railing all but the first coach. This first vehicle had been damaged around the front bogie but it too was dealt with and there matters were left for the time being. Recovery of the tender took place overnight - due to heavy traffic on the line. The locomotive was eventually righted ten days later, that is after the ground had been dug away, rails tied to the wheels and a temporary track laid to haul it back to the end of the loop. Supervising this work was Stephen Townroe, his experience in dealing with the Shawford incident meaning he would be called to attend the not dissimilar Hither Green derailment eight years later.*

28 July 1952 and No. 30747 'Elaine' passes by with an up freight whilst the derailed 'Lord Nelson' continues to display its undersides. The presence of the policeman is interesting , safety, pilfering (this was some years before railway artefacts were considered collectable) or just inquisitive? Where the engine landed was also close to an area of open land popular with walkers, consequently the railway could hardly keep its embarrassment concealed. To make matters worse, Stephen Townroe was then living little more than a few hundred yards from the site, he would probably have been alerted by the sound of detonators long before his telephone rang. Two days later on 30 July the engine was recovered.

All images - S C Towrnroe / R Blencowe collection

From 'THE MECCANO MAGAZINE' for June 1953, intended of course for a younger audience but nevertheless of interest.

Extract from 'Recovering Derailed Locomotives', by S C Townroe

"Steam cranes, with lifting capacities ranging from 36 to 50 tons, are stationed at all large Motive Power Depots. Two such cranes together can re-rail the heaviest locomotives now running on British Railways, provided of course that the load is within reach and that the cranes can stand on firm track. For a full load the radius of the crane jib should not exceed about 20 feet. Owing to the great concentration of weight when lifting, cranes cannot be used on bridges, on light branch lines, or in sidings laid on soft ground.

"After the Weedon accident. in 1951, Pacific No. 46207 *Princess Arthur of Connaught* landed in a field and it was essential to recover it intact, in order to carry out tests to determine why it became derailed. To allow cranes to be used, special foundations had to be laid for them, and

to detect the slightest sign of subsidence while under load, the crane supports were watched through theodolites. In July 1952 Lord Nelson class 4-6-0 No. 30854 *Howard of Effingham* was derailed at Shawford, near Winchester, and lay on its side 15 feet below and 50 feet from the running line. The recovery of this engine intact was effected entirely by the use of a mechanical excavator and a bulldozer.

"First the excavator dug a pit four feet deep alongside the engine wheels, and rails were lashed to the wheels. A timber deck was laid in the pit, and the engine was then rolled upright into it, by jacking from the opposite side of the engine. Meanwhile, the bulldozer cut a slope 240 feet long up the bank, on a gradient of 1 in 13, and a temporary track was laid between the engine and the running line. Finally, the bulldozer's power-operated winch hauled the engine up the bank by means of a hawser and pulley-blocks. The operations took seven working days, and traffic on the main line suffered no interference."

Coincidentally taken by Stephen Townroe four years earlier in 1948, No 35005 waits at the stop signal at the end of the up local line whilst the neighbouring signal is clear for the up main - *exactly* the view that would have been seen by the driver of No. 30854 on his approach. Both signals are seen to be motor operated and were controlled from Shawford Junction signal box. In their final years they were upper quadrant arms.

What would be classified as a 'minor' incident occurred at Southampton (Town Quay) around July 1950 when a 'B4' - the latter just visible ahead of the wagon in the lower view) - and wagon derailed. No cause is given although the presence of sharp curves in the area and plenty of opportunity for obstructions within the flangeways may well have contributed. We cannot know if this was the sum total of the derailed stock, unaffected vehicles possibly having been drawn clear, but the impression is gained that the wagon was being propelled and when it became derailed dragged the back end of the locomotive into a slew with it. Alongside is the breakdown crane, but it may well have been that jacks and slewing would be sufficient to effect recovery. S C Towrnroe / R Blencowe collection

SOUTHAMPTON DOCKS - February 1950

'Battle of Britain' No. 34072

Sometime around February 1950, No. 34072 *'257 Squadron'* 'fell-off' whilst negotiating a particularly sharp curve within the docks at Southampton. (An even sharper curve may be discerned on the extreme left.)

The exact point in the docks where this occurred is not reported, although from the curvature seen it is reasonable to conclude this took place in the Eastern, or older, part of the docks. With no official report available, the cause is not reported and thus a degree of detective work is called for.

Using the photographs as the only clues, there is no obvious evidence of mechanical defect and we are thus left with two potential causes: track defect - again the track appears in reasonable condition with no relaying or repairs evident - or human error. Now whether this was error in the form of slightly too high a speed or the engine had been routed on to a line too sharp for its wheelbase is also not reported, but, from the view above there is no obvious damage to any rail chairs* which does then tend to imply speed was extremely slow and so not a contributory factor, the engine having been brought to a halt almost immediately the derailment was noted. Consequently the most likely cause must be that of the engine being on a line unsuitable for its size. (* There is a slight scuff mark on the top and outside edge of the rail as indicated, but only for a very short distance. Note: there does not appear to be any similar scuff mark, nor rail-chair damage, behind the bogie wheels or to the rear of the front drivers all of which are also derailed. Thus it would seem the engine managed to traverse the curve until the curvature was such that there was insufficient flexibility by the time the centre pair of wheels reached the critical point at which stage the whole front of the engine came off with what would have been a resounding jolt. The only thing we cannot be certain of is whether there was anything on the opposite side of the locomotive that was a contributory factor.)

Consider too the absence of a tail-lamp, so unless this has been removed, the presence of at least one route / duty number disc confirms the loco had been travelling towards what, from the view on page 83 - may well have been a spring loaded turnout. The actual rails give the appearance of a siding and not a running line, for in the opposite direction at least there is no form of facing point lock. (Possibly part of a run-round loop?)

The breakdown crane and gang are in attendance, including at least one 'bowler hat'. From the check-rail in the foreground of the page 83 view, it may well have been considered that the crane itself was - due to its own wheelbase - unable to approach in the ideal position which would have been head-on - so once again giving credence to the assumption the loco had been set on the 'wrong road'. So we now have the crane alongside, not an ideal position for a front lift, but these men would know they were doing and also know the ability of the crane, regardless of the crane's theoretical rated maximum lift of just 35 tons against the engine's 86 tons. The stout packing under the stabilisers will be noted as will the 'runner' for the crane visible ahead.

So it was a case of lift the front end and gently place it back on the rails, hopefully without having to disconnect the tender drawbar. Then presumably, reverse / pull the loco back the way it had come: to do otherwise, in view of the checkrail previously mentioned, would be to tempt providence just a bit too much. The lack of any visible exhaust from No. 34072 means it may have remained in its compromising position for some little time beforehand.

One final thought, might No. 34072 have been sent this way due to its normal route being temporarily unavailable? There would have been a certain irony had that indeed been the case.

S C Towrnroe / R Blencowe collection

SOUTH CROYDON - 24 October 1947

'3SUB' No. 1770 plus two other 3-car sets, and '4LAV' No. 2926 plus one other 4-car set.

Above - The remains of the rear of Haywards Heath train and front of the Tattenham Corner service. It was never established if the brakes had been applied prior to impact. Apart from the obvious stock damage, around 120 yards of track was destroyed on the up main whilst debris caused similar damage to the down main.

The rear end collision at South Croydon on 24 October 1947 was one of three accidents involving fatalities to passengers that occurred in the last few months of private ownership. (The others were at Herne Hill and Motspur Park in November 1947.)

Seen in hindsight the facts are, and as might be expected, simply told. The morning was one of typical dense autumnal fog, the collision made worse that it occurred at 8.37 am, almost the height of the rush hour, and involved two packed trains - and in the words of the inspecting officer Lieut. Col. A H L Mount (assisted in the investigation by Brigadier C A Langley) - that were "overcrowded".

The services were the 8.04 am Tattenham Corner to London Bridge, consisting three 3-car sets having seating for 750 persons but carrying 1,000 persons and the 7.33 am Haywards Heath to London Bridge, consisting of two 4-car sets. This could seat 536 passengers but was carrying 750. Regretfully 32 fatalities resulted and 183 persons were injured, 41 being detained in hospital. Amongst the fatalities was the

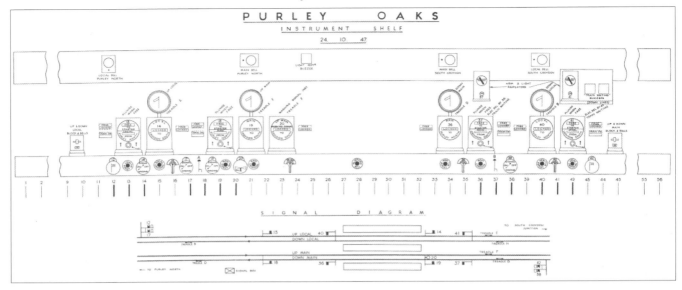

driver of the service from Tattenham Corner.

The collision occurred as the train from Haywards Heath was legitimately passing the home signal for South Croydon Junction at slow speed, having been checked by the associated distant displaying caution. At this point it was struck in the rear by the train from Tattenham Corner which was running under clear signals. This latter event having been allowed to occur in consequence of the signalman at Purley Oaks forgetting the first train and using his release key to free the Sykes system. A momentary lapse which would have terrible consequences.

The signalman in question was in fact graded as a 'Porter/Signalman' but had been passed out as competent to work the signal box five months earlier. The inspector who authorised him as such recalled warning him to use the release key "like a red-hot poker and to treat it as such". It was also reported that there been occasions in the previous period when legitimate use had been made of the key due to genuine failures.

But what happened on that morning was that further up the line delays had occurred, prompting the signalman in the rear to enquire by phone of his colleague what was happening ahead. Upon receiving this the Purley Oaks man appears to have been panicked into thinking a failure had occurred as his instrument still showed 'Locked'. It was of course rightly locked as the Hayward's Heath train was still in section and not in any way because of a failure of the release treadle - as was sometimes the case with the Sykes system. Due to the intensity of traffic no booking was undertaken at Purley Oaks (which action might also have acted as a reminder), whilst the fog was the final factor in preventing a visual indication of the situation outside. (The provision of the Sykes system also absolved a driver from carrying out 'Rule 55' when it would otherwise be required.)

The recommendations of the enquiry were logical and succinct. Regardless of the perceived ability of the man involved it must be questioned whether it was appropriate to put a signalman of limited experience in a busy main line box - even if was in effect no more than a break-section box. Additionally there was the very logical observation that before a release key was used guidance should be sought from the men in the boxes on either side. Here the trouble was that each man would invariably respect each other, and as came out in the enquiry, was loath to question let alone criticise the method of operating by his neighbour.

The final words on this tragedy are best left to the men who were acting as 'fog-men' that fateful morning. Lengthman Langridge was at the distant signal where he estimated visibility was 20-30 yards. As the Haywards Heath train passed the distant had been at caution, a detonator was exploded and he exhibited a yellow hand-signal. Less than two minutes later the distant was lowered and the Tattenham Corner train passed at about 40 mph. His colleague, Lengthman Tipper was on duty at the South Croydon station distant signals - these were positioned on the same post as the South Croydon Junction home signals. This man agreed visibility was no more than about 20 yards, the Haywards Heath train passing under a clear indication from the distant about 15 mph. It was during the time the Haywards Heath train ran between these two signals that Signal/Porter Hillier made his fatal mistake, which notwithstanding an impact speed of perhaps 25 mph, was to result in terrible carnage. Used properly the Sykes system should have aided safety. By over-riding its principal safeguard it created a situation where trains and passengers were moving almost without any safeguard, apart from the vigilance of the man at the front, and he had been hampered by something totally out of anyone's control - the visibility.

Not surprisingly the severity of the accident plus the need to recover casualties meant all four lines were closed to traffic. Even so the up local line was opened three hours later and the down local by 4.00 pm. The main lines were cleared and restored for service at 10.30 am the following day.

STAINES - 9 August 1957

'700' No. 30688 and 2 x 4 car EPB sets: Nos. 5225 and 5144.

The accident at Staines was a simple yet sad case of what would later be termed the, 'ting-ting and away we go' syndrome. Complacency paid a part and resulted in the 12.24 pm Staines to Waterloo service leaving its departure station (at Staines, what had been two separate four-car trains had been combined into the one eight-car train) without the driver having first satisfied himself that the starting signal was 'off'. It was not. And the reason the starting signal was 'on': the signalman at Staines Central was legitimately allowing a light engine to cross from the up loop to the down main line under the authority of a shunting signal.

Apart from complicity by the motorman, the station staff in giving the 'right-away' might also be considered culpable whilst the guard too was required by the rules to similarly check the indication of the signal. The Inspecting officer however absolved these individuals by confirming the ultimate responsibility still lay with the driver, who, shortly after starting away was faced with an obstruction which with its tender weighed 86 tons and was moving slowly towards him. The point of impact was estimated to have been just 188 yards from his departure point.

The accelerating prowess of an EMU also came into play, coupled with a falling gradient of 1 in 511, the final difficulties being the EMU was traversing a left hand curve with a road overbridge carrying the Kingston Road

above the track so as to hinder further any advance view the motorman may have had from his left hand driving position.

As a result the electric train accelerated to about 28 mph when the stationary steam engine was seen, although the motorman immediately shut off power and the emergency brake was applied, speed was still around 20 mph at the point of collision.

One hope might have remained. A relief clerk was travelling on the train who noted the train pass the starting signal at danger but did not act to pull the communication cord. Brig. Langley who investigated the event regarded this man as an unreliable witness and under the circumstances did not consider his lack of action worthy of criticism.

Unfortunately the other men involved, the driver and fireman of the light engine, signalman, a shunter in the signal box and the signalbox lad, all saw the events unfolding but were powerless to have any control on the outcome in the few seconds available to them.

There were 70 passengers on board the electric train, 12 of whom were reported as suffering minor injuries including shock. The motorman was lucky to escape with cuts and bruises whilst the driver of No. 30688 broke a leg and the fireman was reported with unspecified, but believed slight, injuries.

The leading motor coach, S14450S, was badly

damaged, but believed to have been later repaired, whilst several windows were broken together with other 'superficial' damage in other parts of the train.

Unfortunately the impact damage to No. 30688 was terminal, the frames twisted as well as the more obvious damage to the front buffer beam and cab. Consequently the engine was officially withdrawn in September.

No illustrations have come to light showing the electric sets involved although a glimpse of the cab of the front set (number unknown) may be seen in on the previous page.

Below - The rerailed No 30688 - even the numberplate suffered - awaits its fate. Yet again, but as was typical for the time, every effort was made to clear the wreckage and restore services. Breakdown cranes from Feltham and Nine Elms were in attendance by 2.00 pm, the lines cleared five hours later and normal services resumed at 8.16 pm. Assisted no doubt by only minimal damage to track and signalling, the weather was also fine and dry.

Photos - T Wright and unknown.

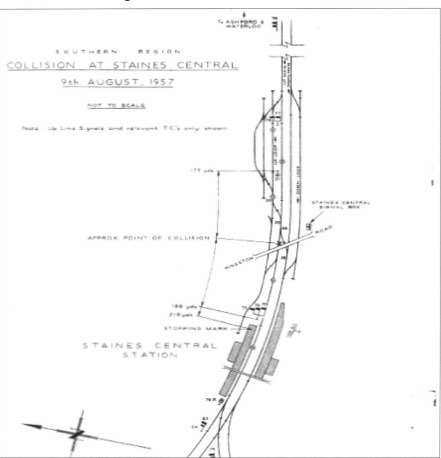

SOUTHERN REGION
COLLISION AT STAINES CENTRAL
9th AUGUST, 1957

NOT TO SCALE

Note. Up Line Signals and relevant T.C.'s only shown

APPROX POINT OF COLLISION

STAINES CENTRAL STATION

'S15' No. 502

In late June 1946, 'S15' 4-6-0 failed to stop at the end of the up loop at Wallers Ash (between Winchester and Micheldever) coming to grief in soft ground opposite Weston signal box - this controlled the north end of the loop. (The location has always been known as the 'Wallers Ash loops' although the two signal boxes were respectively 'Wallers Ash' at the south end and 'Weston' at the north end.) Here No. 502 remained in soft ground until arrangements could be made for recovery. According to Bill Bishop's recollection, apart from the locomotive

running through the sand-drag and ending up in a field, there were wagons piled all round blocking all four lines. This is not seen from the images although from the lower view on this page it is apparent that some vehicles further down the train, and not necessarily immediately behind the tender had come to grief. There is also some indication of what may well be wagon under-frames in the trees alongside the derailed tender. We know also that the brake van at the rear had been derailed. Once these vehicles had been cleared away sufficiently, the train was drawn back to restore the up and down main lines - the down loop being unaffected. In the view lower left on page 89, single line working is in force, the Pilotman seen ready to dismount from No. 21C15 as it approaches Weston signal box. Again part of the culprit train is in place, which implies this view may have been taken shortly after the arrival of the Eastleigh breakdown crane - at the time of just 20ton capacity - and which was then restricted as to what it was able to clear. Three lines were available for normal traffic until recovery of the engine which took place the following weekend.

S C Towrnroe / R Blencowe collection.

WATERLOO - 10 June 1947

'Merchant Navy' No. 21C8 and '4-COR' set No. 3154

Little is known of the collision that occurred at Waterloo on 10 June 1947 other than that which may be gleaned from the actual images. What facts do survive indicate No. 21C8 *'Orient Line'* rammed a stationary 4-COR set in Platform 13. That basically is it, for there is seemingly no reference to the occurrence in any of the contemporary railway periodicals nor has a copy of any accident report or internal investigation been located.

John Fry in his book 'Bulleid Power' refers to the engine having been working an up West of England service and this could then explain the presence of the coaches from the train behind - they seem to be in the same platform but this is not 100% certain. Details of any injuries are also unknown whilst without further information it is also impossible to apportion blame. The railway workers staring opposite present an interesting spectacle.

The images were kindly submitted by Eddie Barnes with prints made by David Flemings.

(Interestingly on the negative packet, the date was recorded as 10 July. However, reference to the Eastleigh Works records shows No 21C8 arrived for repair 'following collision damage' on 18 June. Fully repaired, it was restored to traffic on 30 August.)

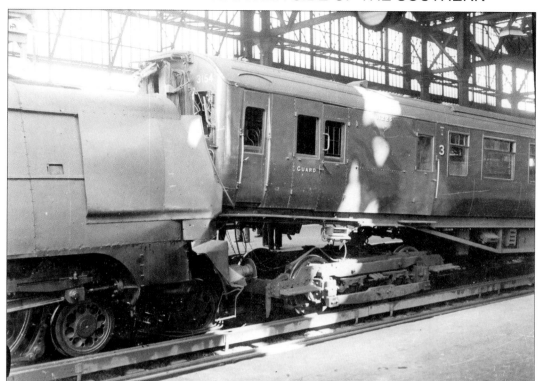

On these and the next page we see further views of the occasion, the image opposite top on page 94 is interesting due to the number of men inspecting the results - visible between the bogie and solebar. Page 94 lower right No. 21C8, is seen in the Eastleigh works yard, obviously turned since the accident and with the rods disconnected having been towed. The single headcode disc may have been part of a Bournemouth or West of England working.

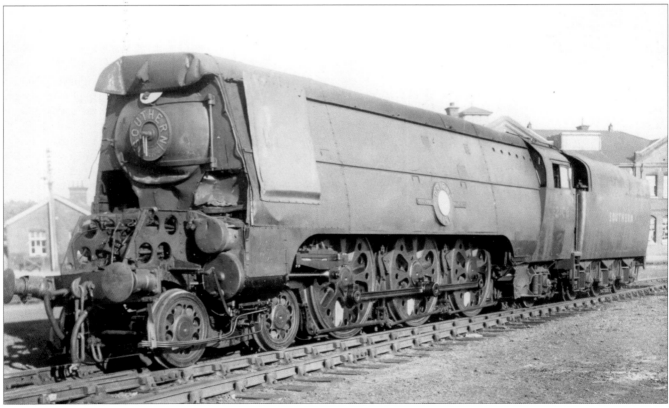

WATERLOO - 11 April 1960

'West Country' No. 34040 and 2 x 4 Car 'EMU' sets

Waterloo April 1960 was a simple, yet sad case of a driver running past a stop signal and coming into violent collision with another object - in this case the tender of a steam engine. Sadly the driver involved died as a result. Why the accident occurred was never explained, sudden illness, signal error, mechanical defect, all were ruled out.

The collision happened at 5.26 pm, so right in the middle of the rush-hour. The steam engine (No. 34040 had arrived in Platform 14 at the head of the 1.25 pm from Weymouth. After the coaches had been removed it was first shunted into Platform 10 before being cleared to depart for Nine Elms) was legitimately crossing the path of the approaching 8-car 4.38pm Effingham Junction to Waterloo train which latter service should have waited at the relevant signal showing 'red'. Instead its driver continued on, smashing pointwork and turning into the path of the converging steam engine running tender first bound for Nine Elms. The distance between the EMU passing the signal at danger and the point of collision was just 195 yards, the two workings converging at an estimated speed of between 32 and 37 mph.

It was a case of 'immovable force and irresistible object'. Something had to give, and that was the cab and front end of the EMU in which the motorman perished. As at Borough Market in January the previous year, exhaustive tests were carried out on the signalling but no defect was found and in the same way the signalmen were adamant the route had not been set for the arriving train and then altered. The damage to the front end of the EMU meant it was not possible to say with certainty if the brakes had been applied on the EMU just before the accident, but the guard and another driver, the latter travelling as a passenger in the front coach, were certain this had not been the case. The guard of the incoming EMU was however criticised for not noticing his driver was proceeding against a 'red'. Possibly at the very last moment the driver of the electric train may have realised something was wrong for the crew of the steam engine recalled hearing a whistle blown, probably the last human act by Motorman Charles.

In the illustration taken of Hercules Road, Lambeth, passengers in the now stranded electric service await release - minor telescoping will also be noticed between the first and second coaches. There were about 100 passengers on the train, medical services were quickly on the scene and arranged for 12 to be transferred to hospital, all were released after treatment. Two others were given first aid at Waterloo. Normal working was in operation by 5.45 am the next day.

WATERLOO - 28 September 1966

BR 'Standard Class 2' No. 82023 and '2-HAL' set No. 2626

The head on collision just outside Waterloo on 28 September 1966 has already been reported on fully in Issue No. 2 of 'The Southern Way'. Little in the way of further information and no new documentary evidence has come to light relative to the collision although what is new are the three images in this work - two on this page and one as the frontispiece.

(In 'Southern Way No 2' it was reported that the electric unit had either been a Windsor local or empty set destined for Wimbledon Park. The latter working can now be confirmed, partly because had this been a passenger train there would likely be reference to an official enquiry, there is none, whilst in addition the frontispiece view shows a tail lamp carried by the EMU. The official withdrawal date for No. 82023 in direct consequence of the collision may also now be reported as October 1966.)

Illustrations courtesy Andy Gibbs / Pete Beyer

WEST CROYDON - 5 November 1922

West Croydon - yes - 5 November 1922 - possibly. There is some similarity with the accident that occurred at the same location some years earlier in 1902 but this is reported as having involved solely a passenger train, yet here there are clearly goods vehicles involved. Was this then an incorrectly reported date, or even a second accident that occurred alongside the first. Suggestion would be welcome!

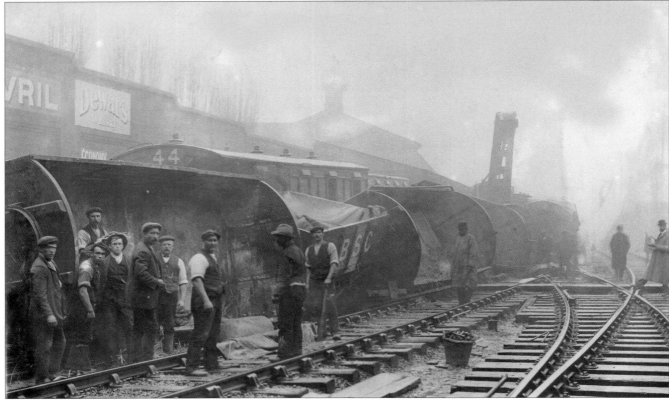

WIMBLEDON - November 1952

Conundrum time - again! The two images on this page were kindly submitted to *'Southern Way'* by Les Darbyshire some little time ago. At that period there was every intention in using them in one of the regular issues but when the opportunity came to produce this particular volume clearly this was their rightful home.

But they do pose a puzzler which despite much searching has to date yielded no answers.

The commentary is then best left to Les himself, "Here are the photos I mentioned of a 'King Arthur' that had got itself in difficulties. Alas, having lost most of my records, I don't know which particular Arthur it was, nor the exact date. I think it was October or November 1952 - certainly it was a very foggy and cold day..

"The location is clear though, just west of Wimbledon station under the footbridge that crosses the line there. My father had a railway allotment alongside the West Croydon line a couple of hundred yards from the main line, and I often took a break from helping him and did a bit of train spotting from this bridge. On this occasion I found the loco in trouble and the breakdown crane in attendance, so ran the mile or so each way home to fetch my camera, and this is the result."

Unidentified 'King Arthur'.

Thus, any information would be most welcome, all we have been able to come with is No. 30768 reported as being fitted with a new left hand cylinder in the summer of 1953. Was this the engine? Was the cylinder so damaged as to warrant a replacement, and assuming the date given by Les is correct, why did it take some months for the repair to be authorised and then carried out?

'Gladstone' No. 172

About 9.25 am on 13 November 1922 the late running (due to fog) 8.42 am Coulsdon to Victoria passenger train was derailed at Windmill Bridge Junction, near Croydon. The engine and first three of the eight coach train came off the line just as the service passed over a worked diamond crossing set for the wrong direction. Damage to the locomotive and stock was limited and luckily there were no injuries.

The cause was unfortunate. This and another Victoria-bound service had been accepted, quite legitimately by the signalman at Windmill Bridge Junction. He set the road for both of these believing the train described on the up main line to be that of the second, Brighton to Victoria service, which although also running late, was to have priority.

He was then advised from his colleague in the rear that the lines on which the two trains were on were in fact incorrect and the Brighton working was in fact going to approach him on the local line. Intending to re-set the route, he was interrupted part way by a telephone call. No matter, there was still no danger as all signals had been restored to danger and fog signalman were on duty. It was only when the driver of the Coulsdon service missed the relevant stop signal that the fact the signalman had not completed re-setting the road became a problem, the train ran through the junction at slow speed with the switched diamonds not set and resulted in derailment seen. Fortunately the prompt action of a ground fogman at the signal box succeeded in stopping the approaching Brighton train before it ploughed into the wreckage.